Primary Colors

and Other Stories

Barbara Croft

Graphics by R. W. Scholes

Minnesota Voices Project Number 45

NEW RIVERS PRESS 1991

PS
3553
R 536
Pn 4
1991

"Beautiful Belle" was the first prize winner in fiction in the Iowa Arts Council Literary Awards competition for 1990. Our thanks to the Iowa Arts Council for permission to include it in this collection. Three of the stories in *Primary Colors and Other Stories* have previously appeared in somewhat different versions, in *The Kenyon Review* and *Calapooya Collage 11*. New Rivers wishes to thank the editors of these reviews for their permission to reprint the stories here.

The author wishes to extend special thanks to Vivian Vie Balfour, C. W. Truesdale, and K. Maehr of New Rivers Press.

Primary Colors and Other Stories has been published with the aid of grants from the Jerome Foundation, the Arts Development Fund of the United Arts Council, the Beverly J. and John A. Rollwagen Fund of the Minneapolis Foundation, Cray Research Foundation, the Elizabeth A. Hale Fund of the Minneapolis Foundation, the First Bank System Foundation, Liberty State Bank, the Star Tribune / Cowles Media Company, the Tennant Company Foundation, the Valspar Corporation, and the National Endowment for the Arts (with funds appropriated by the Congress of the United States). New Rivers also wishes to thank the Minnesota Non-Profits Assistance Fund for its invaluable support.

New Rivers Press books are distributed by

The Talman Company
150-5th Avenue
New York, NY 10011

Bookslinger
2402 University Avenue
St. Paul, MN 55114

Primary Colors and Other Stories has been manufactured in the United States of America for New Rivers Press (C. W. Truesdale, Editor / Publisher), 420 N. 5th Street, Suite 910, Minneapolis, MN 55401, in a first edition of 1,500.

25916308

For Norman

CONTENTS

The Mosasaur	1
The Ragpicker's Boy	5
A Little Piece of Star	13
Blue Horses	18
Primary Colors	23
Groder and The Blind Man	33
Searching for Singleman	39
Turning Blue	50
Cats and Dogs	60
The Bear and The Wedge	65
The Pink Umbrella	77
The Stone	90
Beautiful Belle	100
Someday House	109

PRIMARY COLORS

and Other Stories

The Mosasaur

Carlisle J. Campbell, plowing his field one day near Wymore, Nebraska, turned up a bone the size and shape of an axhead, one of many, graduated in size, that formed the tail of a mosasaur.

"Carlisle, what in the world?" his wife said, eyeing the thing with mistrust.

"I found it," Campbell said, rotating the ancient bone above his dinner plate. "Peculiar, ain't it?"

Campbell did not know what sort of toy he might have by the tail, but he was not the sort of man to leave questions unanswered. Taking a spade and a large, wooden box, he returned to the field the next day and began to dig. Whatever was sleeping beneath the dry, black topsoil of Nebraska was near the surface, nearer than anybody would have guessed.

A man of no formal education, Campbell nevertheless proceeded with the instincts of a trained archeologist. A common garden rake, he eventually found, worked best to peel the earth back gently, just the way a mother eases the quilt from her sleeping child, the way a man might slip the hide from a hog, butchering.

Bone after bone popped up, each one bigger or smaller than the first, and then a wondrously-sculpted shoulder blade appeared, so exotic and strangely beautiful that it stopped Carlisle J. Campbell in his work for a full half hour.

◊

"Carlisle, what in the world?" his wife said, irritated more and more each day that Campbell spent at the bone site. Livestock went untended while Campbell fussed and fretted over a long-dead

1

monster, she called it, old bones. Chores left undone, land left half-plowed. It was just like a man, Mrs. Campbell thought, to be derailed by such a simple thing. Bones. Why, the earth was full of them.

Campbell coaxed his wife into the wagon — it was 1932, but they didn't own a car — and drove her out to the field to see the bone shape sprawled, gently curving, on the land.

"It sort of makes you wonder, don't it?" Campbell remarked to his wife.

"Cover them up," she said.

◊

Campbell worked to free the reposing serpent, spinebone by spinebone, down to the tail tip wedge a half-inch long. Risen to the surface and seeming to drift there, its size surprised him. The delicate oval rib cage was like a cell, big enough for a man to hide in. Sun and shadow would dapple him there, dreaming, while a cool wind sang through the bones.

"I don't know what in the world you're thinking of," Mrs. Campbell said.

◊

Seventy million years ago, Nebraska was a sea. Giant mosasaurs swam in its depths, and pteranodon — flying reptiles — ruled the skies. Carlisle Campbell studied the fierce eye sockets, the sleek, smiling jaws with their rows of triangular teeth and imagined the bones fleshed out to match the picture that Dr. Van Orsdale from the university was showing him.

"Sea serpent," Van Orsdale said. "That would be the common name. A large, eel-like creature — oh, say 35 feet long — but with strong front paddles, like fins, for swimming. They were monstrous. This one's still a baby, perhaps two-thirds the adult length. Very common near the end of the Cretaceous Period."

Campbell and Van Orsdale, lost in thought, stood side by side at the bone site. Each man in his own way heard the sea, saw the flash of bright water.

◊

"Did he offer you anything for it?" Campbell's wife asked him later.

"It ain't for sale," Campbell said.

◇

Campbell collected the bones and brought them home. He stored them in the tool shed and thought about them. Sometimes, late at night, thinking about how the bones gleamed in the darkness, he almost agreed with his wife. Better to cover them up again and get on with things. It was almost time to harvest. But then he thought of the shoulder blade, the way it curved like a question mark, the way the ribs made a cage, and he knew he could never let go of the bones.

Brooding over the bones one day he idly fitted a broad front paddle together. Five-fingered and grasping, it seemed to be reaching out, just like a man's own hand. Maybe it was that, some recognition, that started Campbell fitting bone to bone.

Neighboring farmers thought Carlisle Campbell strange, assembling a sea serpent in his shed. "It's sorcery," Garfield Winsome said. "It's downright, dad-blamed demonology."

Some said Carlisle Campbell had just the sort of mind a homeless, zillion-year-old baby mosasaur would choose, but others said it was just coincidence that brought the monster to lie in Campbell's field instead of their own. Mrs. Campbell's sister agreed with Mrs. Campbell; and the banker, Mr. Folwell, said it was interesting, but not the sort of thing he could lend hard cash on.

Campbell didn't care. He assembled the bones and studied them. Strung out on the dirt floor of the tool shed, they told him something about himself, but not enough. He scrambled them with the toe of his boot, dumped them back in the box, shook the box and tossed them down on the dirt again. Campbell assembled the bones.

Meanwhile, his farm faltered, finally failed — she knew it would — and Campbell sold the land for half its worth. On the day the auctioneer arrived, Campbell was in the tool shed.

"I hope you're happy," Mrs. Campbell said at supper.

Campbell told her he had decided to move to Iowa. He had already, he said, begun to pack.

"Carlisle," Mrs. Campbell said. "You're not taking *those*?"

◊

In Iowa, things went from bad to worse. Totally preoccupied with the bones by then, Campbell let everything go, including Mrs. Campbell, who moved to Kansas City to take a job with the telephone company.

Campbell's hair and fingernails grew long. His eyes took on an empty look. The teeth rotted out of his head. Visitors — some on business and others just curious — approached the Carlisle Campbell farm with awe, then mild anxiety, then dread. Finally, no one came around at all.

Through general neglect of health and diet, Carlisle J. Campbell shrank to little more than a skeleton himself. A day's work was fitting the bones together. Their intricacy assembled filled his soul, and the curve of a single bone could sweep his mind clean of all other thought.

Campbell knew the bones like the back of his hand; their shape was memory, beyond sight. At last, caught up in the bone cage of his mind, he didn't need them anymore; and like a blind man Brailling a final message, Campbell assembled the bones for one last time and glued them to the east side of the barn.

They were visible from the road for many years, bleaching against the rotting wood like an advertisement for Red Man. Campbell hoped that motorists passing by would see the bones and reflect. He hoped that they would serve as a reminder of how easily monsters can enter into our lives — and how easily, once they do, we can find a place for them.

The Ragpicker's Boy

The ragpicker's son was a lean, quick boy, tall and blue eyed and proud. His hands were slender and strong veined, holding the reins, and my brother Jim thought he must be the luckiest kid in the world because it was his job, his privilege, to drive the wagon. He sat on the high seat, lapping up sunlight, alone, while his father, a grizzled, dark-faced, shambling man, fussed and muttered over the backyard trash.

They had two horses, a black and an ivory white one, pulling together in ancient harness that was cobbled up with wire where the brass was gone. Probably the boy had a saddle at home and rode the white horse anytime he liked. That's what Jim said. Or, he hunted rabbits; he'd have a dog, too, of course. And, probably, the saddle had some silver on it — not a lot — but there'd be some bits of silver and some on the bridle, too, because that's how we thought then it always was when a boy owned a horse, two horses, all his own.

We had only bicycles and cement.

The black was an old Roman-nose; he looked like a mule. But, the white one looked to us like a cowboy's horse. From where we stood, the black seemed no more than an out-of-shape shadow cast by the white, while that big white horse shone in the sun just like fresh milk. Even in the shade, he still seemed to shine, to throw back the sunlight he'd caught in himself — like the moon.

Grandma used to say the human mind was full of tunnels: that a thought begun in innocence wound backward or forward in time, turned on itself, wormlike, that thoughts wove mazes that held our lives together. I still think of the horse and the moon together. And I think of Jim.

This was the time my father owned the hardware store, and Grandma still lived with us in the gray house on Washington Street, long before Jim went away. The war was over, though it had meant little to us as children. All we knew was that somehow, somewhere we could hardly imagine existing, some unspeakable evil had arisen, fought savagely with the mild-eyed GI good guys from Texas and Brooklyn, and retreated at last before a nebulous, good-natured personage my father referred to unfailingly as "Uncle Sam."

Evil was over, finished, felled before good intentions and a pure heart like a giant in a fairy tale, and an age of goodness was on the way. I remember Jim, heaping dead leaves and empty cardboard cartons on an autumn bonfire. Burning Hitler's house. Or, sitting on the back stoop, his hands jammed deep in his overall pockets, his eyes anxious for the wagon and the big white horse to start down the alley.

We didn't pull up clumps of grass for the ragpicker's horses like we did for Old Bill, the milk horse — we didn't dare — or dust their legs with rocks to make them stamp. We didn't follow that wagon. There was something spooky and strange about those people, especially the old man.

Mornings, you could hear them coming first: the patient plod of the horses' hooves like a ticking clock, and then the creak of the harness, the rattling wheels. The crash of tin cans sang down the crooked alley: Old Mrs. Snyder's, the Moores' house, the Bensons' and ours. Through the backyard saplings, the lilacs and hollyhocks, the gray-colored, weather-warped wagon appeared every morning.

We hid behind the mulberry bush to hear the singing Tennessee twang of their voices. They said such funny things sometimes, that old man and his boy. But, we were afraid of the old man; he was the devil himself. He had huge, clutching hands and powerful arms, and his eyes were red and watery and wild.

He'd walk from house to house, stopping at every one, lighting on each trash bin like a big black fly. Sometimes he'd knock on the lid of it first for luck, and then he'd begin. Sorting slowly over the rags and bottles, the broken this and the useless that, his heavy, work-thick hands had a delicate grace. Like patient black spiders, like things with a life of their own, his hands moved slowly. They hypnotized us, inspiring an awe for what could be bought and sold, or turned up — by chance, by luck — and used again.

For the old man was a firm believer in luck. He had a hunch that something would be there, and he had all the time in the world to find his treasure. Not even seeming to use his eyes, but Brailling like a blind man, he weighed and valued everything in the bin, taking his time, not overlooking a thing.

Then — crash — he'd slam the lid down, turn and throw what he'd found in the wagon, and they'd move on. But first, he'd cuss us a good one for the string-saving Christians we were.

The boy had the same hawker's eye and the same steady, fisherman's patience his father had, but he was not like his father or like us. Fourteen perhaps, but already a man, he drove the team with a clear and high disdain. Our bikes and roller skates, our tame city lives didn't interest him; why should they? We were children, and he didn't see us at all. Or, when he did choose to see us, watching from the bushes, jealous and horse crazy, he'd brag about the team, especially the white.

"This here horse ain't no pullin' horse," he'd call to us, meaning the white. "This here horse is a ridin' horse."

He was our hero then, especially Jim's. Staring out, all slouchy proud, every bit as though he saw a horizon, the ragpicker's son gave some serious thought to things. And, if his eyes hit hard on a back board fence, we never saw him flinch. When, breaking into his own first, fragile manhood, Jim fought Daddy, growing distant and sullen, and Mama said (mistaking Jim, still thinking of her baby) they would give him away to the ragpicker, he could go be the ragpicker's boy, Jim said he didn't care. The fence that kept the ragpicker's boy on the outside kept Jim in, and his heart was in some magic place, high on the wagon seat, a ragpicker's boy. Like us girls, he worshipped the life that old man and his boy led, and wondered would they take anything from our bin.

One day my sister Julia and I were watching the clouds, making up stories about the shapes they had and naming the ponies and dogs we never would own, when we heard the wagon and ran for the mulberry bush. We barely made it; he almost saw us that time.

7

The old man was wearing a heavy black coat, although it was already summer, and a dirty gray dress hat pulled low on his brow. We could hardly see his face, but we heard him grumbling as he poked around, and we watched his coattail swing back and forth, gently whipping his legs.

There was nothing at our house; we never threw anything out. If it could be patched or mended, handed down or used again somehow, we saved it. We weren't poor people, Mama said, but a dime was a dime to us. There was no use looking in our bin, but he always did, just on the off chance we'd slip up and let something valuable, even a pop bottle, by. But that almost never happened, and that day there was nothing.

"Hard times," he muttered, "hard times. Harder for some than others."

He slammed the lid down just as he always did, but this time he didn't move on. He just stood there, looking at the house. And then he looked at the wagon and back at the house.

When he looked again at the house, it made us look too. It was nothing special, just the house to us, with curtains breathing in and out at the windows and a fresh white wash swaying on the line. We could hear Mama bustling around in the kitchen and smell the bacony soapsuds of breakfast dishes. Somewhere a radio played in and out of the wind, muffled and then clear and then muffled again. It was a small, neat house with the kitchen in the back. Worn wooden steps led out to the bare, grassless yard where we played and on to a low, weed-lined fence. That's where we put the trash, just beyond the fence.

"Hard times," he was still saying. "Yes sir, hard times."

He saw the bucket all along, of course, left out where Daddy'd forgot it, and he must have known it wasn't for him to take. So he was just pretending to notice it, to deliberate for a while was it worth the taking, which it was, of course; it was brand new. And then, when he thought nobody was watching him, he snatched it up and hurried on down the alley. And the boy drove after his father same as usual.

Julia — she was the oldest — ran for Mama, and sharp thrills of outrage ran all through us. "Mama, they're taking the bucket," she cried in a whisper. "They're taking Daddy's new bucket!"

"What? Oh, those . . ." Mama hissed. Boiling out the back door, she wiped her hands on her dress hem, biting her lip. She peered anxiously over the fence.

"Run, tell Jim to get it back," she said.

"Mama says for you to get it back, Jim," Julia screeched, running back to us all out of breath.

We knew, of course, he couldn't possibly do it. Grandma used to say that old man was the devil himself. Julia said he could cast spells and make you bark like a dog if he wanted to. She said she saw him do it once, and they lived in a cave full of bones. If he ever caught hold of you, you'd be a goner, sure.

So, we followed the wagon all right, but just going its pace. Any moment we could run for it if he saw us. When they stopped, we stopped, and when they moved again, we moved again, stalking them like Indians. Julia and I stepped timidly, huddled behind bushes when we felt the need, but Jim walked straight down the middle, never taking his eyes off the high wagon seat. We could see the old man's coattail swaying up ahead, first in the shade of the fences and then in the sun and then in the shade again, and we heard the wagon moving slowly along behind him.

Julia kept poking Jim and whispering, "Go ahead, Jim, go ahead." But, he couldn't do anything. I didn't want him to.

When they got to the end of our alley, we knew the old man would jump up on the wagon. He'd whip the horses into a trot, and they'd head up Clark Street, and they'd be gone for good then and the bucket with them. But, we couldn't do anything. We kept hanging back.

Pretty soon they knew we were following them, and the old man started to scowl even more than ever. My heart was going like mad and my legs felt hollow, I was so scared, and I thought, poor Jim, he's got to do it.

This time when the wagon stopped, the ragpicker's son jumped down. He was shorter than we had thought, heavier. When he saw us looking at him, he looked away, pretending to help his father who was cussing to beat the band now, he was so mad. The trash cans rattled like thunder under the old man's hands, spooking the horses and shaking the birds from the low-branched crabapple trees. Julia and I were scared to death and about to run when

9

suddenly the old man whirled around on us, shouting, "What y'all want?"

He was looking right at us now, his eyes on fire, and we looked back, all of us stopped stone still. The world grew quiet. Only the wind still moved, twirling the leaves on the trees and stirring up sunlight. Little beams of it danced on his coat like coins. Finally, he broke his eyes away and said, "Get on out the road 'fore you hurt yourselves."

We couldn't move or talk; we couldn't do anything, and the longer we stood there, watching, the madder he got. He was hopping mad by then, but the boy came up, and he asked us this time, softer, "What y'all want?" and Jim blurted out, "You got my daddy's bucket."

I wanted to run sure then; the old man was coming, growling at us, "We ain't got nothin' but trash."

Julia pointed at the bucket; he still had it in his hand and he said, "This? Your daddy threw this out."

"Well, didn't he?"

Julia was all through being brave, and I couldn't speak at all. "Well, didn't he?" There was no answer.

"You, boy, speak up, didn't he throw it out?"

I could hardly hear him, but Jim said, "No, sir."

That old man, he changed then right away. His eyes melted and his voice went soft. He licked his lips and said, "You're mistaken, boy. We found this bucket, me and my boy, throwed out. You don't think we'd steal it, do you?"

"No, sir."

"Well, I should hope not."

He smiled and hunkered down beside Jim, as if he were going to explain to him just how it was. He was so close to us now I could smell his coat; it smelled like rotting trees. He held Jim's arm tightly. His teeth were black.

"No, sir," he said. "We just happened along and seen it, and I says to my boy here, no use that goin' to waste, seein's how them folks throwed it out. Ain't that where you always throw things out, out back the fence?"

Jim had to nod.

"Course it is," he said. "I thought as much."

10

His voice sang on and on in Jim's ear, coaxing and bluffing and joking him along. Julia was backing away, like an ice cake melting, but I was still watching them talk because Jim was my brother, and something I could not stop or even name was happening to him. Jim stared, not seeing, at the ground, making the toe of his shoe go in dusty circles. Tears were forming in his eyes — I didn't want to see it — and he was listening hard.

"So you see, you're mistaken, boy," the old man was still talking when the tears began to race down my brother's face. I can still see them, cutting like acid through his light summer tan. Perhaps, lost now in unspeakable sadness, he thought once of reaching his hand out to stroke the big, white horse, but he did not. Nobody moved, and the wind, light and shifting, stirred aimlessly in the dust.

I'd never seen the horses that close up. They were sweaty and galled in spots where the wire had cut them. Little trickles of blood attracted the flies. The white one hated the harness and several times, while I watched, his flesh ran in shivers and he stamped. Close up, he looked dirty and broken, taller but no better than the black with which he was matched. He was no riding horse; even I could see that.

A Little Piece of Star

In 1934 a meteorite about the size of a softball fell from the sky over Kearney, Nebraska, where my grandfather was living, and pierced the roof of his 1932 Packard. And although it was just, as my grandmother described it, a *little* piece of star, it convinced my grandfather that he had a destiny.

He reacted immediately and in a way that changed his life and ours forever. He did the unthinkable. He sold the farm. *Sold his land for a piece of sky,* my father always said, bitterly. My father was the older of Grandfather's two sons and might have had the family farm for his portion instead of a narrow desk in the claims department at Mutual of Omaha, where he worked for forty-eight years.

The meterorite — it was not a star, though we always called it one — did not stop when it came through the roof, but steamed on through the upholstery on the driver's side, leaving a hole the size of a dinner plate and embedding itself in the ground underneath the car to a depth of about six inches.

If my grandfather had been sitting in the car at the time, he would, of course, have been killed.

"But I wasn't," he said.

Or the thing might have come down on the passenger side, where my grandmother, Millie, sat.

"But it didn't," my grandfather said.

In addition to attesting to my grandfather's manifest destiny, the hole on the driver's side revealed to him a simple wisdom few men have, the knowledge that he was *alive* and that the situation could change at any moment.

Although I was not there to enjoy it, the event made my grandfather and his family local celebrities. He was marshal that year of the Fourth of July parade and — suspended over the meteorite hole in the driver's seat by a one-by-twelve pine board — he drove down the main street of Kearney in the Packard, on the hood of which a flimsy gilt star had been fastened. My father, who rode in the back seat, said the cheering crowds embarrassed him, but to the townspeople, this accolade did not seem unwarranted. After all, they reasoned, the thing could just as well have come down on another man's car or somewhere out in the sand hills with no one there to observe it.

"But it didn't," my grandfather said.

It came down, people said, like a finger from heaven. It intended my grandfather, and it would have been, therefore, a kind of cosmic insult to ignore it.

The money from the sale of the farm financed Grandfather's college education. He was thirty-nine when he moved his family to Lincoln and enrolled at the University of Nebraska, the first one in his family to have attempted higher education. Not surprisingly, he studied astronomy. And poetry, and art. It was a useless course of study and, perversely, just what he should have done. I like to think that, in the back of his mind, he knew it, too, and that he turned so utterly from a sensible path for no better reason than that meteor had in plunging toward his Packard: for the clear and sacred unreasonableness of the thing.

Understand, too, that my grandfather's family was not suffering, financially, in Nebraska. He did, after all, own a two-year-old Packard. Given that, and the year — it was 1934, not a propitious time to be burning bridges — Millie's objections, which were numerous and clearly stated, made a great deal of sense. Nevertheless, my grandfather was determined to follow his star.

With two young children and a wife to support, however, he soon found that his money did not go far. He was forced to quit school in his sophomore year and work. He sold hardware for a while, and — this never surprised me — he was good at it.

He re-enrolled two years later, then quit, then re-entered. This went on for several years until at the age of forty-six he quit school altogether. Millie had been ill for some time — she died in 1941, just on the brink of the war. The children by then were both nearly grown; my father was eighteen and already working for Mutual of Omaha. There didn't seem much point in going on.

He was no wiser, Grandfather said, than when he had started out for Lincoln seven years earlier, no more enlightened about his destiny. His knowledge of astronomy had taught him, in the end, no more than that meteors were dust.

All of this was a long time ago, as I said. And the only practical outcome of it all, from my point of view, was that for the first fifteen years of my life I was forbidden by my father to read anything but my school books and the *Omaha World Herald*. Words — words like "destiny" and "star" — could make a man — as my father claimed his father had — throw his life away.

Fiction was strictly forbidden, as was poetry and any sort of speculative essay. Having had a near and painful lesson in what can happen when a man begins to imagine, my father wanted for me what he himself had had: a steady income and an orderly existence. Only he wanted me to like it, as he had not; he wanted me to be free of the tension he felt as a man forever caught between earth and sky.

Grandfather lived with us until he died at the age of seventy-four in 1969. He still studied astronomy and made it his yearly ritual to observe the splendid meteor showers that splash across the Nebraska sky every August. He tented out in our back yard with Peterson's *Field Guide to the Stars and Planets* and an elaborate assortment of war surplus camping equipment, and, unbeknownst to my father, I camped out with him, sneaking out to the tent after midnight when the best show was just about to begin. By then the earth had rotated enough to show its flat Nebraska face to the stars and we were traveling into them rather than seeing them from the side like fenceposts slipping by outside a car window. I was nine, and it seemed to me that I could almost feel the wind from the stars on my face as they rushed past.

Grandfather had a German telescope — an ancient wood and brass thing with a huge lens that reflected all the colors of the spectrum — set up on a tripod and pointed toward the northeast. What he was aiming to catch was the Perseids shower, the remnants of the famous Swift-Tuttle III comet of 1862.

"We'll be plowing into them now, Willie," he told me. "The earth is a ship."

He liked this metaphor and had said it to me so often that it was no longer necessary for him to add "and it sails through the universe." He had star maps and books and globes to illustrate this point, how the planets move, but I was content with the poetry. I imagined a square-rigger, a figurehead looking something like Millie breasting the waves, stars falling to either side of the prow in dazzling whitecaps and Father in our wake, bent over his desk.

Father kept his father on a tight allowance. More from spite than for economic reasons, he limited Grandfather as much as he could, treating him like the child he believed him to be. Grandfather's poverty restricted him to one pound of Borkum Riff a month, a lesser quantity and quality than he used to smoke in the palmy days before the meteorite when he ordered a specially blended perique mixture from Iwan Ries in Chicago. He smoked on ceremonial occasions and when he was with me, the only person in the family who actually liked the smell of a pipe.

He lit it now, and we leaned back on a stack of worn-out sofa pillows we had scavenged from the basement. The meteorite that had started all the trouble lay on the blanket between us, indistinguishable to most people from an ordinary rock. We looked up at the stars, not as clear as they would have been in the absolute dark of the farm back in Kearney, but distinct and distinctly beautiful, and my grandfather talked about astronomy, starting with the Chinese in A.D. 36 and moving forward to ourselves in the back yard in Omaha at a pace that took all night.

They came as quick streaks, sometimes one a minute, and seemed to emanate from one point. I thought of them alternately as the blaze from some celestial battle, the spark of a kiss, the trail of a firebird. I imagined something splendid in being "showered" by heaven, and I'll admit my faith in magnificence faltered a little when my grandfather told me that the stars were dust. I felt as though I had slipped on a cosmic banana peel, had the celestial rug pulled from under my feet. But Grandfather said, after all, all living is a betrayal.

And then, of course, he died. I was fourteen or so, already forgetting the magnificence of heaven in the daily cares of earth. I blush to admit that I was not deeply moved when he died. I was busy with living. It may help you to understand if I mention simply that I grew up to be an internal auditor, not an astronomer, that I still live in Omaha, and I do not own a telescope.

My grandfather was not the first man, I'm sure, who failed to figure out why he was placed on earth, and since the dent in my education is, as I said, the only clear outcome of the event, there's no reason why I should be telling you this story, no reason why I should think you might want to hear it. It's just that, viewing my life at this point as a long and far from dramatic process of having my spirit broken, I like to remember what my grandmother said — about the little piece of star — and to picture again my grandfather, sitting outside his tent, endlessly polishing the rainbow lens of his telescope and waiting, waiting for something glorious to descend upon him.

Blue Horses

"Why should there be blue horses?" the man said.

The woman clipped pictures of the world's great works of art. She'd done it all her life, even back in Hungary as a child, before the trouble, before she'd ever met him, before everything. She couldn't remember when she hadn't done it. Just pictures, out of magazines, things that struck her.

"Because they just are," she said. "Blue. Why should you be a man with a black moustache?"

The man shoved her picture album back across the dining room table toward her. "Blue horses," he said.

"If she likes them, she likes them," the other woman said, the blond woman. "Why should you care?" She gulped her wine down. "Why do you care what she does?"

"I don't care."

"Yes, Gabor," the blond woman said. "Yes, you do."

They were in Gabor's house: Gabor and Anna, his wife, and Gabor's younger brother, Miklos, and the blond woman he wanted to marry. They had just finished dinner.

Gabor rose slowly and walked around the table to stand directly behind his wife. He reached over her shoulder and flipped the album open.

"So." He gave the album three sharp taps with his index finger, then rocked back on his heels and folded his short, thick arms over his chest. "Educate me."

"Gabor."

"I want to know," the man said, "Miss Art Collector."

Wearily, the woman thumbed through the album and stopped

at the picture of the blue horses. "Look," she said, "curves."

"So?"

She took his hand in hers and traced the curves of the horses. "They're for thinking," she said, "thinking new." She tapped her temple with her left index finger. "Forms."

"But, forms of horses," the man said. He tapped his head, too, and smiled for the others. "Hey? Forms of horses, yes? Am I right?"

The woman closed the album.

"Am I right? Anna? Tell me."

"Yes, you're right."

"They love to be right, hey?" the blond woman said. "Men, I mean. Don't they?"

Anna said nothing.

"Rather be right than rich." The blond filled her glass again.

"And women," Gabor's brother said. "They know everything."

"Keep talking," the blond woman said. She was not Hungarian. "You're getting smarter."

Gabor drew Anna up from the chair and cuddled her close from behind, pinning her arms to her sides and nuzzling her neck. "Why do you like them?" he said. "Hey, why do you like them, rabbit, why?"

She struggled. "Don't," she said. The horses stirred restlessly in the shadows. She heard the stamping of their hooves in the hallway.

"I'm tired," she said.

"Good," Gabor said. The brother laughed.

"No, tired. I'm tired." She struggled free. "I'm going to bed."

◊

Why should there be blue horses? Why should there be a man to ask about it? Always. They just are. Why should there be a fat woman, no longer pretty, who tries to explain?

Anna went into the tiny back bedroom and closed the door behind her. The room was cool and quiet. She put on her cotton nightgown and climbed into the high double bed. Blue horses, blue horses, their rumps smooth and glossy as the phrase itself, their necks proud.

She wound the round black Big Ben clock by her bed and turned out the light. Laughter filtered in to her from the living room.

She heard Gabor's voice raised above the others.

There is a plain where time drips from . . . something, a tree branch, perhaps. She couldn't remember. He, Gabor, hated that picture, too, time dripping from a tree on an empty plain, the sense of something dying. In her mind, blue horses entered timidly, one or two at first, then a dozen or more, at the back of the picture. Their eyes were wary, and their feet danced, restless, on the bleak flats. *Because we are*, they whispered.

The horses circled in the background, nosing the dirt. She heard their breath — *we are* — come and go like the sea. Then, suddenly, they caught some scent on the air, spun, all the horses together now as one, gathered force and charged the length of the empty landscape, bursting through, the picture destroyed as a shaft of light swept the room like a lighthouse beacon.

"It's dark in here."

The door slammed shut again.

"Of course."

She heard him fumbling in the dark. She heard the whoosh of fabric as he removed his trousers, saw quick, blue friction sparks twinkle. Coins spilled on the hardwood floor.

"Damn." She heard him drop to his knees. "Get the light," he said.

"Leave it."

"Get the light."

She switched on the lamp. Gabor, in his underwear, was down on all fours pursuing nickels and dimes beneath the furniture. "This always happens," he said.

"Take the money out of your pockets first."

"I know, I know."

"You don't know."

"I forget."

He crawled into the bed on the other side, making it rock like a small boat.

"I didn't hear them go," she said, turning out the light again.

The man said nothing.

"Well?"

"Well?"

"Is he going to marry her?" she said.

"I told him no," the man said. "I said no." He peeled his

wristwatch off and laid it carefully on the nightstand.

"But he loves her," she said.

"He can love somebody else," he said. "She talks too much, that one. Canadian. She's no good for him."

Gabor crawled on top of Anna and pulled her nightgown up above her waist. "He needs somebody older," he said, pulling his underwear off and dropping it over the edge of the bed. "Not flighty like that one." He kneaded Anna's heavy breasts and began to make love.

The bed rocked, squeaking like saddle harness as Gabor worked. He squeezed his eyes shut and began to sweat. Anna stared at the ceiling where blue horses marched, dragging their heavy haunches and winking down at her with huge, comic eyes. Their feet were round, the size of dinner plates, and they lifted and fell like sluggish machinery.

As a bride, she used to take hold of Gabor's fingers and draw them to her, trying to teach him to rotate just the tips of his fingers inside her. Blue horses. His fingers would stir her briefly, then wander away, and the blunt utility of him would reassert itself.

Now, she lay still, listening to the squeaking rhythm as he plunged on, rocking the bed with his labor, and she thought: *Why should there be blue horses? Why should there be blue horses?*

Primary Colors

In Florence, Michael insisted Anne buy something for herself. They strolled the Ponte Vecchio, looking at cameos, lapis, malachite and gold. They looked at marble inlays along the Via Vespucci; they looked at leather handbags and silk scarves.

In the end, she settled for a few picture postcards and a gaudy paperbound book called *Art Treasures of Florence* that she bought in the Piazza della Signoria for 4,000 lire. All she really wanted was to see the David, over and over — singular and blinding white at the end of the corridor of slaves. She was in love with the slope of the shoulders, the gentle, proud turn of the head. She kept coming back to it, circling, letting some new angle surprise her, some slightly changed cast of light.

They had been married for only a few months when a series of hard-edge color studies won Michael a fellowship — six months in Italy. She borrowed from her father to go with him. They lived in one cramped room and spent every morning at the Uffizi, swimming in art and sea-green marble. They napped in the afternoon beneath the cool blue cypress trees. They shopped the Straw Market and bought wide-brimmed Van Gogh hats woven of coarse rush. They bought raw coconut, ice cold, from the street vendors and wandered the maze of dark, narrow streets. At night, they ate cheap, heavy tourist meals, drank Chianti and talked about art. Anne even began to draw again herself — intricate pencil studies of the twisted olive trees and splashy color sketches of the city, the people. She window-shopped and listened to Michael talk.

Art. The city of art. They lived like artists then. Flying back from Rome two years ago, they hadn't talked about the future —

where to live, what to do. It hadn't seemed necessary. They thought six months in Italy would last them the rest of their lives.

Now it was Iowa again and a small farm — just an acreage, really — they'd been able to rent cheaply while Michael taught at a nearby college. Now it was spring again, or, more precisely, the tense prelude to spring when the days glow strangely with a thin artificial sunlight and nothing seems quite ready to grow.

Maybe, Anne thought, when Michael was established, she'd get a studio of her own and do some serious work again. That's what her father kept urging her to do. When he wrote to her from some midwestern Holiday Inn — he traveled for a big electronics firm in Cedar Rapids — he always signed his cards the same way: "Keep your dreams."

Anne watched Michael through the kitchen window, chopping wood at the block. He wore a blood-red sweatshirt that seemed defiant against the early green, and his short, thick body was tight with energy. The farm had seemed like a good move at first, but the isolation and the empty Iowa landscape weren't right for him. He was used to Iowa City, to people and the reinforcement he got from other artists. The flat, raw fields depressed him, and for weeks he did almost nothing but sit curled in an armchair, reading. When he did work, he simply repeated the subjects and style that had earned him praise at school.

Then a fellow teacher, John Lester, persuaded Michael to try to paint outdoors — something he'd never done before — and it forced a change in his work. The two men made field trips into the countryside, hiking for miles sometimes, painting and talking, and slowly Michael began to understand the subtle planes of the land, the depths that shifting light created on the shallow contours of the fields. He was particularly attracted to a low, limestone cliffside about fifteen miles north of the Interstate, and he painted it over and over in different lights, from different perspectives.

The new work made Michael quarrelsome, and he and Anne fought openly for the first time in their lives. He didn't want her advice, only her mute, unceasing admiration. Even John Lester was eventually excluded from his vision.

"Technically, Lester's okay," Michael told Anne, "but his work is slack, effeminate."

He became moody and defensive. "It's not the same for you," he said to her once when she had offered some slight analysis of his work. "You're not a serious painter."

One of the worst things to Anne was the way he began to guard his materials. They had always shared before, borrowing paints and brushes without asking. Now Michael often accused her of using things up. "It's not like you really need them," he said once. "I *need* these things. I need them to paint." Eventually he moved his studio out to the barn and bought a lock for the door — to keep out prowlers, he said.

And eventually, too, there was a pointless, brutal quarrel with John Lester. It happened over dinner one night, and quiet, good-natured John pushed back from the table, rose slowly, said goodby and walked out.

"He'll never be any good," Michael told Anne; he was furious. "You'll never be any good," he shouted out the doorway as John's car shot away in the darkness. He turned to Anne. "And you," he said. "You. You like him, don't you?"

Anne was worried enough to call her father.

"Stay away from him," he said. He made it sound easy.

"How can I?"

"Just do it."

◊

Anne watched Michael select a log from the wood pile and balance it uneasily on end, holding it untouched with an outstretched hand the way a man commands a dog to stay. The log seemed almost obedient. Then lifting the ax suddenly, he swung, and the dark log split open in one clean wound, exposing fine-grained wood as pale as flesh.

He was different now than he had been six years ago, when they had both been students at Iowa City and Michael had first been "promising" as a painter. Lying in bed, drinking beer and making love, looking at art books together — Picasso, Kandinsky, Georgia O'Keeffe — he had explained to Anne what, at first, she had not been able to see for herself: How the color reinforces the form, how the artist works within the almost arbitrary dimensions of the canvas, accepting them and yet, in a very controlled way, fighting out against the restrictions, forcing the image beyond the pictorial surface. "Limitlessness," he said, playing the stubby "i" sounds against the hissing "s." "Distance and time." In great art, he told her, there is a vastness, all possibilities actual, waiting, held in endless suspension.

Still, art is illusion — the impression of depth on a flat surface, the impression of life and movement in dead stone. The virgin mother of the Pieta could never really hold her dead son in her arms. Anne thought of that piece when she thought of holding Michael, his heavy shoulders heaving, crying inconsolably and with an almost comic sobbing because some work of his he believed in had not been noticed at a student show. She hadn't be able to comfort him — this was four or five years ago — and as it turned out, it hadn't mattered. An hour later he was talking painting at the reception, a plastic glass of cheap Chablis in his hand, while she helped the other wives and girlfriends pick up the dirty paper plates and the crumpled napkins.

◊

"Almost ready," she called as he stomped through the doorway, his arms full of firewood.

"I want to wash up," he said.

She turned the fire down under the bacon. "What time's he coming?"

"I'm not sure." He was trying hard to be casual. "He said early. Nine, nine-thirty." He couldn't quite look at her.

He ran up the stairs, and she heard his voice filter down from the bathroom. "I think I'll show him the drawings first."

"Fine," she hollered back.

"I think they're a better introduction, kind of a prelude to what I'm doing now."

"Yes," she yelled back, fumbling. "I think you're right."

She drained the bacon, put the toast in and prayed. *Please let it be all right.* He had called Ryan Pierce out of some grandstand, all-or-nothing impulse to show in Chicago before he was thirty. Ego. Michael was good and he knew it. It gave him a sort of power.

That was the difference between them, perhaps. Her art was cramped, personal, obedient to fact. Or she dealt in fantasy, the other side of the coin, the rebellion of obedience which, left ungoverned, could carry her far away from the matter-of-fact, sunlit world of duty where she lived most of the time. Michael's art was a different thing altogether, a willfulness that merged his personal life with the tradition and enforced his vision. He *made* his life into art by force of will, insisting on his uniqueness so intensely that, ironically, the merely personal burned away, leaving pure artifact, symbols that seemed universal.

As Anne broke eggs into a large white bowl, she thought of the casualness of Pierce's letter. He'd "drop by" to have a look at Michael's work, he wrote, his sprawling, loose penmanship contrasting almost arrogantly with the enforced dignity of the textured, buff-colored paper, the prim logo of his posh gallery. Power was casual, she was coming to see, almost random.

◊

Ryan Pierce's Mercedes pulled into the lane about noon, and Anne watched through the window as Michael walked out from the studio, squinting into the sunlight. The two men shook hands.

She refilled her coffee cup and sat down at the kitchen table. Pierce was short, pudgy, balding, a bit of a dandy in a pearl gray suit. He didn't seem big enough to wield the power he apparently had.

She thought of her father, a big man with steel gray hair and blunt, efficient hands like Michael's. "Did you do what I said?" he had asked her lightly over the phone.

"Do what you said? I didn't even know what you meant," Anne had told him. "Anyway, it's working out."

When her father spoke again, he sounded tired. "Why do you think your mother and I broke up?"

She didn't like to talk to him about this.

"Do you think it was because I wasn't successful enough?"

"Dad," she said. It was ridiculous. Her father was a classic workaholic. Nobody fought harder for success, and after many setbacks and a few outright failures, he'd made it. Two weeks after he got his last big promotion, her mother had filed for divorce.

"I did it to her," he had said. "I made her go."

"Dad."

"I used her up, Baby," he had said. "I used her all up. There wasn't anything left."

Anne had been surprised to find herself crying. "I don't feel used up," she had said.

"Keep painting," her father had said. "Promise me."

Once — long before she'd met Michael — she'd dreamed of a big show herself. Her hair had been longer then, lighter. She'd worn antique jewelry and Danskins and worn-out jeans on which she'd embroidered the story of her life in primary colors. She had had a kind of gift — that's what someone had called it — a talent for organic forms.

Once she'd done a series of studies inspired by the wriggling cells of life seen through a microscope, and they'd been highly praised. She'd worked mostly in watercolor, letting the paint spread out on the wet, toothed paper, then barely reining it in with a few lines of ink; but someone had told her — perhaps it was Michael — that she really should work in oils. Serious artists were judged by their large canvases, their oils, and while everyone realized that watercolor was a very difficult medium, perhaps even more difficult than oil, it was too introspective, too delicate. It wouldn't gain her much recognition among serious critics.

She thought of some of the studies she'd done in Florence, watercolor sketches of the city at evening, just at the rising of the moon when light rimmed the dome and etched the delicate tracings of the bridges. She had tried then for a precision of line and bold color, but if she were to work them over now — again in water-color — she'd want to stress the purity of the light, that whiteness, soften the color. She would let the paint wander a bit, as she had in the microscope studies. In a sense, it would be what was not there, what she left out, that would evoke the mood most power-fully. The violent, heavy impasto of Michael's early work and the high-gloss super-realism he had evolved to weren't the only ways to work.

Male voices on the gravel driveway jerked her out of thought. "Well, it's hard to say," Ryan Pierce was talking. "There might be a time slot next year. Or, you could enter something in the general show. Many begin there."

They came in from the sunlight, Pierce still talking and Michael trailing behind him, his face empty.

"Well, Mrs. Ross," Pierce said. "Your husband is a talented man." He smiled broadly.

Anne smiled back. A dozen responses occurred to her, each one too wifely. Her mind went totally blank, and there was a long, awkward pause.

"I've suggested to Michael," Pierce began uncomfortably, "that he take a little more time to develop his style." Anne looked straight into the dealer's eyes.

"Not that the work isn't good," Pierce went on, edging toward the door. He had his pearl gray hat in his hand.

"I'm not ready," Michael said bluntly, letting the words fall like blows on Pierce and his wife.

"Michael," Pierce crooned. "We just don't want to rush things. Believe me, that's always a mistake. Your work is promising, very promising indeed. And, in a year or two, when you've had more time, I could take another look."

Michael said nothing.

"Believe me," Pierce said. "That really would be best."

"Would you like some coffee?" Anne asked suddenly. Stupid, stupid. A typical wife's solution.

"Sorry, no, Mrs. Ross," Pierce said. "I'm late already. Promised to stop by the college and talk with John Lester while I'm out this way. He has a few things to show me."

With one hand on the door knob, Pierce stopped.

"What's this?" he asked.

Hanging in the hallway next to the coatrack was a small watercolor landscape Anne had done years ago. Pierce noted the signature. "Your work, Mrs. Ross?"

Anne glanced nervously at Michael. He wasn't smiling.

"It's really nothing," she said. "Just a little study."

"Now, now, dear," Michael boomed. "Don't be so modest."

"Michael," she said.

29

"You may be the real artist in the family, after all," he said. "Don't you think so, Pierce?"

"He's kidding," Anne said.

"No. No, I'm not." Michael pulled the picture off the wall and pretended to study it. "Such honesty. Such freshness," he said. He turned on Pierce. "Maybe you'd like to arrange a show for Anne. Maybe the effeminate is more to your taste."

Pierce's face flamed with anger; he pulled the door wide open and started out. "I mean, since I'm not *ready*," Michael shouted after him. Pierce slammed the door.

"Faggot," Michael hissed. He stared at Anne, his face dark and wooden, his eyes cold. Then, without a word, he turned his back on her and walked away.

◊

Anne had tried, half-heartedly, to flag Pierce down before he left, but she had caught only a final glimpse of his face, frozen with rage, behind the gleaming window of the Mercedes. Then the car turned, flashed sharply in the sun, sailed effortlessly through the curve in the lane, took the little rise by the gate and was gone, leaving the hedgerow weaving helplessly in its wake.

As she entered the hallway again, she heard Michael slam the bedroom door upstairs.

"Michael?" she called.

She began to climb the stairs, calling "Michael?" There was no answer.

When she reached the landing, she knew instinctively that the door was locked. Beyond it, she heard the sound of a window closing, shades being drawn.

"Michael," she said, "Michael, open the door."

She heard his muffled voice, but she couldn't make out the words. "Michael," she said. "What is it?"

Silence seemed to seep out under the door, pooling at her feet like something cold and obscene. He would not speak.

"He *liked* them," she yelled. "He said you were *talented*."

His silence now rushed out at her in waves. She could almost feel it wash against her ankles. It cut deep; it burned. He had used this weapon before.

She sank down on the worn hall carpet and leaned her cheek against the cool enamel woodwork. In an hour or so, Michael would open the door. He would be quiet and moody. They'd have an early dinner, maybe drive into town for a movie. Later, in the old iron bed she had rescued from the Salvation Army thrift store, they would make love. In a day or two, Michael would grab her hat from the coatrack and do a funny imitation of Pierce, and she would laugh, glad to have him back. Then they would never talk about it again.

The hall was dark and quiet. She closed her eyes, hardly thinking about Michael. She could see moonlight in her mind, how it brushed the limbs of trees, how the faintest hint of color could define it. Shapes rose up in her imagination, hungry as caged animals, and drove her husband from her thoughts. Once or twice she thought she heard him crying in the dark room beyond the door, but the sound seemed foreign and very far away.

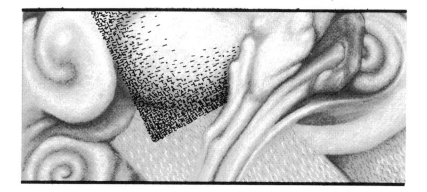

Groder and The Blind Man

The Blind Man hears space. The Blind Man sees time. The Blind Man knows you're there when you barely know yourself, and he scares the hell out of Groder.

Tapping along, The Blind Man comes on like death, relentless. Groder flattens himself against the wall of the Save-U-More. He sucks his belly in.

No use. The white cane finds him, prods him a little.

"Ouch!"

"Sorry."

The Blind Man shuffles on.

◊

Groder hears The Blind Man approaching as he peers through the window of the Christian Science Reading Room and ducks into the doorway, but The Blind Man homes in on him.

"Ouch!"

"Sorry."

The Blind Man goes inside.

Groder sees the man again coming out of a movie house, wearing dark glasses, Groder decides, in order not to be recognized. The Blind Man's in the office, waiting, when Groder shows up to apply for unemployment. He detects him, by his slim, white cane, concealed in a polling station and again in a public urinal, secluded behind the door.

◊

Groder shivers at the eastbound bus stop with a thin, green bottle of Yugoslavian Riesling under his arm. Undoubtedly, Loraine will have Kraft's Monterey Jack and the little square wheat crackers Groder likes, and the white cheese and the white wine will be just right together while they're watching *60 Minutes.*

Groder lifts his right hand and waves intently at no one in particular, listening for the bus money tucked inside his mitten, and running bass beneath the tinkle of the coins is the tap, tap of The Blind Man coming straight down the middle of the sidewalk like bad news.

"Ouch!"

"Sorry."

The Blind Man, Groder now believes, may not really be blind. Even while Groder watches him, he snakes around the bus stop sign, dances lightly off the curb and swings up on the steps of the bus the minute the doors fly open. This is no blind person, Groder decides.

◊

"He's not really blind," Groder tells Loraine. She sits at his feet, painting Mercurochrome on his ankles. A puncture hole the size of a cane tip oozes a rusty-colored blood. Groder does not condone socks, even in the coldest of weather. The feet must breathe.

"You should wear socks," Loraine says, dipping a Q-tip in the bottle. She paints a tiny heart on his instep.

"He's not really blind," Groder says again.

"So?"

"So why's he doing it?"

"Maybe he *feels* blind," she says. Loraine clearly does not grasp the implications.

"It isn't right." Groder jumps to his feet; the Mercurochrome goes flying. "What if everyone did that?"

In the building where Groder's mother lives there is a small black kid named Alonzo who pretends to be deaf. He taps you on the shoulder, and when you turn around he makes his eyes go wide as hubcaps and almost touches but doesn't quite touch his right ear. He gives you a card with many fingers on it: the deaf alphabet. The card explains that Alonzo isn't asking for charity, just a donation, but Groder's mother says she hears him late at night, singing "Deep Purple" and "Moon River" up in his room.

◊

Loraine's Pomeranian has a rare skin disease that requires constant attention. His thick orange hair falls out in patches, and Loraine spreads a slimy pink liquid over the naked skin. Naturally, Groder is not invited to spend the night.

"It wouldn't be any good anyway," she tells him. "My mind wouldn't really be on it." She gives him a kiss that curls his toes, and it's more than enough.

Groder stumbles down the stairs and out into the cold, clear night. Every star is visible. Every sound carries for miles. Groder feels keen and raw as if his puny nerves pulsed with the great and single electric charge of the universe. Sometimes, all undeserving, we are transformed. No longer the bewildered, all-too-material Groder, he is Perception, inhaling all life, digesting all thought. He is MAN unconquerable. His eyes rove territorially down the block and stop at the corner where the last westbound bus sails by, carrying The Blind Man's face framed in a window.

◊

"I'm fed up with it," Groder tells Loraine. A thin trickle of blood ornaments his pale ankle, the fifth wound this week. Caught loitering near the warm spot where the Laundromat vents the dryers, Groder has taken yet another sharp hit to the tarsus.

Loraine bends over Groder's ankle, blowing on the wound to dry the blood. "I'm out of Mercurochrome," she says. "Is Lysol okay?"

Groder calls the police, the county sheriff, the social services office, the area council of churches. No one knows The Blind Man. No one cares. There is no law, he learns, against pretending to be blind. There is, furthermore, no state or federal agency that authenticates visual impairment, except, of course, the Department of Motor Vehicles. Does The Blind Man have a driver's license? Groder doesn't know.

Two days later The Blind Man gets him again, tripping him up this time with the long, white cane as Groder climbs the library steps.

◇

"Are you coming with me or what?" Groder has taken matters into his own hands. He has rented a silver Honda Civic and stands, half in, half out of its open left door, staring at what he believes to be the only woman he'll ever love.

"I'm not sure," Loraine says.

"You realize," Groder tells her, "that this is all symbolic. Highly symbolic."

"I thought it was," she says.

"It's now or never, Loraine."

She climbs reluctantly into the passenger's side, and Groder slips behind the wheel and starts the engine. The car sounds like an electric typewriter, a food processor, a sewing machine. "I should have gotten something bigger," Groder muses.

The car hums down the main street, and Groder settles his shoulders into the silver upholstery. He reaches for Loraine. "There are times, Baby," he says, "when a man's got to know his woman's behind him." He eyes her. "All the way."

Groder cruises the bus stop, the Christian Science Reading Room. No luck. A mental grid of the area's side streets flashes in his mind, and he systematically combs them one by one, trolling along with the Civic in low gear. At Leonard Place, he spots a shabby shuffler in a dark raincoat and his heart beats fast, but it isn't The Blind Man.

"Of course!" Groder thumps his fist on his forehead. "It's Wednesday afternoon."

"And?"

"He'll be at the movies."

He pulls a wide U-turn at the corner and screams back down the street, careening at the intersection and letting the Civic have its head on the straightaway. Loraine clings to the door handle, watching for a chance to jump. "If I can make it by 3:55," Groder says, "I'll nail the son of a bitch."

The Civic flashes by the movie house just as the first squinting afternoon patrons are pushing through the chrome-trimmed double doors. Groder slams the car in reverse and backs into an alley to wait.

36

"I'm getting out." Loraine has one foot on the pavement when Groder spots The Blind Man strolling alone in the winter sunlight, tossing popcorn in the air and catching it deftly in his teeth.

"The bastard." Groder grinds gears; the tires squeal and smoke, spinning for a split second on the cold asphalt, then biting in. The Civic takes off like a shot.

"Keep an eye peeled for cops," Groder yells. But he's alone. Dimly and at great mental distance, the crumpled Loraine-shaped object in his rear-view mirror registers in his mind. Probably just lacerations, Groder thinks.

The Blind Man reaches the corner and waits for the light, a man, to the casual observer, at his ease. Inside The Blind Man's head, however, some slight rearrangement of time and space clicks in and settles like a fallen leaf. As lightly as a woman shakes out a shawl or a man sets his hat, The Blind Man's universe changes, and he is alert, straining for sound.

The Blind Man knows Groder by his demonic smile and perceives his purpose just in time to spin clear of the Civic's cruel fenders speeding past. He turns and runs. Cutting through the parking lot, he vaults a low snow fence and skitters across a frozen yard inches ahead of an irate bulldog. He runs four blocks and his breath is coming hard when he sees a brick wall, scrambles up and over, drops on the other side to a blind alley with a high fence on either side and the Civic at the other end, steaming toward him.

Tough spot.

The car squeals to a stop. "Who the hell are you?" Groder bellows out the window.

The Blind Man cowers, whimpers, "I'm your fate."

"Bull shit."

Groder throws the Civic in reverse and backs up to get a good run at him. The old death machine, what a car. He imagines The Blind Man's bones crunching against the brick wall, his blood pooling on the concrete. He revs up the Civic till it screams.

"Stop, stop." In the mirror, Loraine again, running, waving her arms. No way, feminine principle. A man's gotta do what a man's gotta do. Groder slams the car in low and guns it.

"Groder, stop. Groder."

The car shoots forward. Groder looks back just for an instant, sees her, fragile, running, lovely Loraine, the chance missed. Then forward again, the death mission, the speeding car, The Blind Man, the brick wall.

On impact, The Blind Man flies straight up in the air like an angel, and the nose of the Civic slams under him, hits the wall and crumples. He loops lightly, slow motion, and drops on the silver hood with a hollow thump as Groder, a little surprised, comes flying forward through the windshield. Wet with blood, he meets the staring Blind Man finally eye to eye.

Searching for Singleman

Singleman first appeared when I was writing to Willoughby, although I did not notice the error at the time. "Error" is, of course, a simplification, even a glossing over of what happened.

I did not see that Willoughby's letter was, in fact, addressed to Singleman because the letter was computer generated and, of course, no one really reads computer generated correspondence, assuming — this is the bedrock of electronic applications of this sort — that the computer knows what it's doing.

And it did. It does. I'm convinced of that. Nor was Singleman a glitch. Singleman, I was to find out, was all too real. I use the term loosely.

I did not notice Singleman until Willoughby responded. "I notice you address me as Singleman," his note read. "I'm Willoughby."

I called up the file and checked the correspondence, first spell-checking the letter on the screen — which, strangely, yielded nothing — then actually reading the letter word for word. I found that, though the inside address and mailing label were correctly addressed to Willoughby, the salutation read "Dear Professor Singleman."

Singleman, Singleman. I did not recall the name, but then, since the mailing list was computerized four years ago, I have dropped the habit of remembering names. I opened the database and ordered a global search for Singleman. He (I suppose he could have been a she) was not in the system. I checked the paper backup system, even taking time to flip through the dusty file cards one by one, in case Singleman had been misfiled. The name was not there.

Nor was Singleman listed in the international directory of

sociologists, the American Society of Sociologists graduate school guide, *Who's Who in Sociology,* or Pittman's extensive watershed bibliography in *Twentieth Century American Sociology.* He/she was unknown to my colleagues.

Mysteries do not intrigue me. In fact, as a sociologist, I do not even recognize the existence of mystery. Effects have causes, although they may be obscure, and this principle operates within the context of the complex interactions of populations, i.e., human culture, every bit as tightly as it does within the — to our perspective — restricted world of the amoeba. I decided to ignore the whole matter.

I would have, too, if Singleman had not reappeared a week later, this time in the references of a paper on deviance I was reading. I telephoned the author.

"Who's this Singleman," I said. "I've never heard of him."

"Singleman?" the author replied. "There's no Singleman in my paper. I never heard of him either."

I reminded this young man that I was the editor of *Sociology Today* and that he was an assistant professor in a land grant college and that his tenure decision, I understood, was still pending. I implied that my acceptance of his paper might well have a salutary effect upon the tenure committee's decision.

"There's a Bachman," he said, trying to be helpful.

"But Bachman is not Singleman," I said.

After that, Singleman began to turn up with disturbing frequency. I found him cited in numerous papers. More disturbing, a letter that the department secretary swore she had addressed to the proper person returned unopened, but with Singleman's name (no address) now typed on the envelope and the word, *undeliverable,* stamped over it. I opened it immediately.

The inside address was correct, the contents as I had dictated them, but the letter had obviously been handled, and — conclusive proof — there was a large, muddy thumbprint near the bottom.

I couldn't ignore this any longer, I decided. It would not have been scientific. I took the afternoon off and visited the library, where a young female at the reference desk assisted me in searching for Singleman through the data banks of the nation's top research libraries. It took better than an hour.

"There's not one single man named Singleman," she said finally, smiling.

"That remark is not even remotely amusing," I informed her.

I seemed to be at a dead end, and then, as so often happens in research of this sort, a breakthrough. I was browsing through an out-of-print bookshop right here in Madison when a title in the bargain bin leaped out at me: *A. E. Singleman: The Pioneering Spirit*. I snatched it up.

It was an odd book, half biography, half tribute to a man, a sociologist of sorts, who had been dead for over twenty years but who, apparently, was well ahead of his time in the development of qualitative research — a methodology I have always regarded as unacceptably messy. The author was female, a Gwendolyn Clarkson-Turner, and she lived — amazing chance — only ten miles or so from the university where I teach.

◊

"I was Singleman's pupil," she told me when I went to see her next day. "At Chicago. I was part — a very small part — of the Chicago School. It was terribly exciting for me. I was a young girl, and the movement was just at its height. Of course, by then Dr. Singleman had gone beyond all that." She stopped to draw a deep breath. "The man was . . ."

"Intelligent?" I prompted. I ordinarily never prompt a respondent.

She looked at me with scorn. "I hardly think that covers it," she said.

She was elderly and very formal in manner. I could see I had offended her. "What was it," I asked. "What was it about him that attracted you?"

"I was not '*attracted*,'" she said.

"Intellectually, of course."

Her eyes took on a dreamy look, but she did not speak.

"Ms. Clarkson-Turner," I said.

"Why do you come to me?" Her eyes flashed. "Clearly," she said, "Dr. Singleman has come to you."

I was dumbstruck. "You would scarely have been allowed to continue attending Dr. Singleman's lectures," she said, "with so little ability to apprehend the obvious."

She was right, of course. I had looked for Singleman too far afield. All the while he was right there in my computer.

◊

"It's like any social gathering," Ariel Gatewood said. "It's like a party really."

Ariel Gatewood taught poetry and was described by her students as "ethereal." Rowen, the English department chair, referred to her as "a flake," and opinion generally fluctuated between those two poles. Nevertheless, Ariel Gatewood was exactly the person I needed to reach Singleman. A dabbler in the occult and known, surreptitiously, as a medium, Ariel Gatewood had talked to Yeats on numerous occasions, she claimed.

"It's just so uplifting," she told me. "Until that man Pound shows up."

Holding a seance via computer was not Ms. Gatewood's usual style, but she agreed to help me, and late one night we met at the editorial offices of *Sociology Today* to try what could be done.

"You must not be disappointed," she said, "if we do not succeed at once. The man *is* a sociologist."

She clutched Clarkson-Turner's book and — I have this documented — it began to glow. I switched on my computer and inserted an initialized disk.

"Create a file," Ms. Gatewood said. "Name it Singleman. Maybe he'll come down to inhabit it — they do that sometimes."

I did so, then typed in "Singleman?"

There was no response.

"Dr. Singleman?" I typed. Nothing.

"Let me try," Ariel Gatewood said. "Maybe I can woo him." We joined hands and each put our free hand on top of the computer. It beeped faintly.

"Ohooooo spirit," Ariel Gatewood intoned. "We seek you, the departed spirit of A. E. Singleman." The screen was a dead gray. "I have someone here with me," Ms. Gatewood said, "who badly needs your help."

"I don't need his help," I whispered, "I just want to know who he is."

A pattern appeared on the screen and a menu: file, edit, search, intuit, transcend, generate, transmogrify, expand.

The pattern began to change, flipping rapidly through the computer's repertoire from dots to squiggles to a linear pattern that looked like a brick wall.

"Are you trying to reach us?" Ms. Gatewood asked. A series of quick beeps answered her, then, suddenly, the screen blazed with light so clear and intense that we had to look away. A flicker of light played on the walls, and we heard the keyboard chuckling. When we looked back, the keys were moving, dipping and rising rapidly as if invisible hands were typing upon them. "Are you Mortimer Hockett?" the invisible hands typed out.

"Yes," I typed.

"Mortimer *J*. Hockett?"

"Yes," I typed.

"The sociologist?"

"Oh, for heaven's sake, yes."

"Hi," the machine typed, "I'm A. E. Singleman."

The light subsided, and the computer began to hum. "It's an honor," I typed.

"I have a message," Singleman typed. "For you. That's why I've been causing all the trouble. It's about the work you've been doing. And *my* work."

"My cultural census project?" I typed.

"That, too. But mostly about the journal. I've written a paper I want you to publish."

Singleman died, rather dramatically, Ms. Clarkson-Turner told me, during a T-grouping session in 1968, and the two or three unpublished manuscripts he left were published posthumously.

"It's short," he typed. "I promise."

I didn't know what to say, and Ms. Gatewood came to my rescue. "We understand, spirit," she typed, "that those of you who have crossed over often feel that you have left important tasks undone."

"But a paper twenty years old," I interrupted. "It really won't do. *Sociology Today* is about . . . well, sociology *today*. We could do a retrospective or something."

A period of silence (8.3 sec.) followed; the screen dimmed.

"I'm a genius," Singleman typed out finally. "I don't say that to boast; it's just a fact. I began to read when I was two. My first word was a complete sentence, compound-complex. It was a comment on the nutritive content of oatmeal. I went to UCLA when I was fourteen, the youngest in my class. I played the violin, chess, IQ off the charts. I had my Ph.D. in hand when I was twenty-one."

"No one's disputing . . ." I started to type.

Singleman deleted my words. "All the big schools wanted me," he typed. "I could publish anywhere. I did. Again, I'm not boasting. I'm trying to make a point." The screen dimmed again, then grew bright, like someone taking a deep breath before beginning a complicated explanation.

"Everything I wrote," Singleman went on, "thousands of words, was junk. I really have only one thing to say."

Ms. Gatewood and I looked at one another. "I think he's getting tired," she whispered to me.

"Singleman," I typed. "Could I get back to you?"

"I'm not going anywhere," he typed. The screen went blank.

◊

I'm sure there is no necessity to note that it is not the policy of *Sociology Today* to publish the work of the dead. And this Singleman — an engaging fellow — but who had ever heard of him, other than Gwendolyn Clarkson-Turner, whose judgment was obviously impure?

I explained all this to my wife, Muriel, and she said, "Well, under the circumstances, I don't see what else you can do."

Muriel has the usual biases and thought patterns of her socioeconomic class and age classification — she's forty-six — and, context aside, she is not especially bright.

"What else, what?" I said. "What else but publish him, what else but *not* publish him?"

"What else but what you've done," she said.

"But I haven't done *anything*."

"Oh, haven't you?" she said. "I wasn't listening."

◊

"See here, Singleman," I typed the following night, "I'm afraid I'm going to have to be a little bit hard-nosed about this."

A lone question mark appeared on the screen.

44

"It's a matter of policy," I typed, "not any reflection on your work."
Another question mark, in bold this time.
"Our policy — the policy of the journal — is that we simply do not publish the work of the dead."
A very long pause (13.5 sec.) this time.
"I'm afraid you may have hurt his feelings," Ariel Gatewood said.
"You haven't even read it," Singleman typed slowly.
I explained to him — and this *was* a bit of sophistry on my part — that, if I read the paper, my decision would no longer be impersonal, that is, uncritical. It would then *seem* — although this would not necessarily be the case — that I was rejecting the paper on its merits, or lack of merit. Whereas, in fact, as I had just explained, my decision was entirely objective and based on policy which, of course, in turn was based on (a) academic tradition and (b) the consensus of the *Sociology Today* publications board, for whom, it could be said (with qualifications), I worked.
"Baloney," Singleman typed. The screen went blank.

◊

Meanwhile, my own work was not going well, and I suspected that it would not have been completely without basis to factor in the personal element. I was almost fifty. I had two books out, one very slight that I was not particularly proud of (but that had earned me tenure) and my dissertation, written twenty some years ago when I was more certain than I am now about what the social sciences can reveal. There were articles, too, of course, and I had read at most of the major society meetings. But my role, more and more, it seemed to me, was that of facilitator. I was a panel moderator, a dissertation director, or, in my present role, an editor — someone, in short, who makes things possible for other people.
Muriel, predictably, did not understand why this should distress me. "I'm one, too," she said, "a facilitator. It doesn't bother me."
That she did not appreciate the cultural shaping factor of gender on her self-perception was typical.

◊

"I'm sorry," Singleman typed the next night. "I apologize."
I had nothing to say/type back, and we sat, he and I — I use

all these terms loosely — for some time without communicating. I had found during the second seance that I could reach Dr. Singleman by myself and had told Ariel Gatewood that she no longer need keep me company during these late night conversations.

"I wish . . ." I typed finally.

"What?"

I couldn't put it in words.

"What?"

"I wish that I," I typed, "had something — anything, it could be just one little fact — that I believed in enough, that I wanted to *tell* someone strongly enough . . . well, like you."

"A fact won't do it," Singleman typed. We had argued over the course of the evening about the merits of qualitative vs. quantitative methodology, about constructionism and how, according to Singleman, the multivocality of a dead man's world view, contrary to expectation, deprivileges his stance as an omniscient analyst. We talked about stratification theory and debated the concept of truth as a valorizing defining process in regard to facts and observations and whether the supposed objectivity of the scientist/observer was possible, even desirable, in field work. Singleman's mind was nimble, and he was well-informed; but, at times, I suspected that he doubted every premise of the discipline.

"Tired?" he typed finally.

I hit the space bar once, a code we'd devised between ourselves: one tap for yes, two for no.

"Get some sleep," Singleman typed.

◊

I was, frankly, exhausted by these communications, and I avoided talking with Singleman for almost a week. Then I had one of those days, extremely stressful, and when I did call him up, I was, I'm afraid, a bit edgy.

"You work too hard," he typed. "Take a vacation."

"Sure."

"Take your wife, what's her name?"

"Muriel."

"Take Muriel," he typed. "Go to the islands. A little personal 'interaction,' if you know what I mean." Singleman typed out a line of X's and O's, the hugs and kisses we all used to put on our letters when we were kids. "Palm trees," he typed. "Sun. Those goopy drinks with the little paper umbrellas in them."

"Muriel's not the interaction type," I replied.

"No?"

"Muriel . . ." I typed. "We've been married for many years."

"And?" Singleman typed.

"Well, things change," I typed. He waited. "Or, rather, they cease to change."

Singleman did not reply.

"Of course, we still have a bond," I typed.

"Of course," Singleman typed.

"I love her," I typed unexpectedly.

"And?"

I was thinking of Muriel. It wasn't what I'd call romantic thinking. I just saw her in my mind, the way she always is, neatly dressed and quietly busy at something.

"And?" Singleman typed again.

"Well, I guess I'm surprised," I typed. "I didn't know that about myself, not really."

"And?" Singleman typed. The word hung on the screen.

And, indeed. Throughout my career there had always been something to say, some thought or action that seemed to follow almost automatically, an order, a process, a method. Now I couldn't think of a thing that should logically come next. I kept thinking instead of those drinks with the little umbrellas in them and how cool they must be — I'd never had one — and how they must be made with something sweet, coconut milk and rum perhaps or maybe pineapple juice.

"Singleman, what's the message?" I typed.

At first, I thought he was gone; he took so long to reply. "Mort, you're not going to like it," he typed.

"What is it," I typed. "I want to know."

"I've done it all," Singleman typed, "quantitative, qualitative, statistical analysis. I've interviewed . . ."

"Get to the point."

"And theory. Oi! Constructionist, deconstructionist, post-

47

modern, Marxist, feminist. I dropped acid with Timothy Leary once. Did I tell you that?"

"Singleman."

"I've been around the block."

"WHAT'S THE MESSAGE?" I typed in bold caps.

"The message," Singleman typed, "is that we don't know. The human heart, the mind — totally unpredictable. Thank God," he added.

I was stunned, then angry.

"You come to me, jerk my life out of shape." I was typing fast. "You tell me you have a message — no, *the* message, the message of all time — and you even get me to listen. Drop my work, everything, night after night tapping away at this keyboard. And what's the message? That we don't know?"

"So, life isn't a fountain?" he typed. "Ha, ha. A little joke."

I refused to answer.

"You know that joke?" he typed. "It's an old one."

I refused to be drawn in.

"A man goes looking for the secret of life," he typed. "And he goes to the oldest guru in the world who lives . . ."

"I've heard it," I typed.

So, this is the end of all wisdom, I thought. Ignorance, the happy animal life. A brilliant career, a view from the vantage point of eternity, and the end of it all is the beginning, that we don't know the one thing in life worth knowing.

"I knew it would make you mad," Singleman typed. "It made me mad, too, at first, but when you get used to the idea . . ." I switched him off.

You can do that with machines, just switch them off. I didn't bother to save the file or go through the shutdown procedure, and I don't know what effect that might have had on him. It couldn't have hurt him much; he was already dead. And I had made it clear early in our relationship that I had no intention of publishing his work. Our business was concluded, really; I had no reason to call him again.

Except that, when I got home, I found Muriel, dressed in a kind of red silk oriental thing — not very warm looking — and little else. There was a bottle of Kahlua, unopened, on the kitchen counter and a tray of ice cubes, and I had the impression that someone had just left the house, left in a permanent way. There was no evidence for this, no cigar stub smoldering in an ashtray, nothing that obvious, just a look around my wife's eyes and, of course, the Kahlua. I knew that she had been about to cry when I came in and that now she would not.

"I just wear this thing around the house sometimes," she said, avoiding my eyes. She opened the bottle and poured herself a good-sized drink. "Want some?" she said.

There didn't seem any reason not to join her. Muriel found some soda crackers and a slice or two of American cheese, and we sat down at the kitchen table. I noticed as she drank that deep pucker lines had developed around her lips, like the lines on the lips of much older women who seem to have about them an air of moral severity, and I knew that the lines were formed by pursing the lips, not in arrogance, but against pain. I'd seen this in hospital patients when I had a grant a few years back to study illness and aging. It wasn't included in my data base, of course, but there's a look of pain I have noticed that is almost haughty. And I noticed now, too, that Muriel curved her hand over her mouth as if to hide these lines or something more, and that her hands were beginning to show the dark brown spots of age. But the point of all these observations is that I was seeing *qualitatively*; I was seeing, as Singleman would say, beyond the data.

I would have liked to tell him what I had seen, the connection/distinction between arrogance and pain, and the way that I had discovered it in my wife. But I knew that he was gone, just as Muriel's friend was gone, and that it was just the two of us again, as it always had been. So instead I took her hand. I hadn't done that in years. "Want to hear a joke?" I asked her. "It's an old one."

Turning Blue

On my grandmother's farm in Missouri, just about fifty miles north
of the Arkansas line, the forsythia flowered early in the spring,
and the bluejays fought every morning over the crusts of bread
my grandmother left on the stump in the back yard. Her house
was made of field stone and sat on a hill about ten miles outside
of town. There was a porch swing, and no matter how hot it got,
you could always catch a breeze there.

My grandmother was born in the hill country farther south, a
remote area she called the piney woods, but after she married
Grandfather — I think it was 1921 — they moved north to Al-
bion, and she lived there all her life.

Grandfather was what they call a gentleman farmer. He ran a
few head of cattle and kept enough land to pasture his Tennessee
Walker and a buttermilk saddle mare for my grandmother — which
she rarely rode — but he spent more time at the feed store swap-
ping stories with the other men than he ever did running the farm.
Gram raised chickens — and five children — and tended her garden
and canned and sewed and played the ebony Steinway piano Grand-
father bought for her as a wedding present. She kept the place
together.

Grandma made apple dolls, wizened little people carved from
withered apples. In her later years, the years that I can remember,
she began to look a little like an apple doll herself, her face wrinkled
and seamed like pine tree bark. She sold the dolls to tourists in
Albion for pin money, but she kept a few back, nestled in a hand-
woven wooden basket, for me and my cousins.

I don't suppose those dolls are still made today, or at least, not in the same way. I imagine the hill people are gone, and I don't guess anyone makes those wooden baskets anymore either, not by stripping the soft, ivory pulp from a sapling early in spring and soaking the wood and weaving it, flaws and knots and all, by hand.

Gram collected glass, American pressed glass mostly and some paperweights. She lined her windows with colored goblets on glass shelves, and in the morning when the sun came through, the carpet was spattered with blue and rose and amethyst. She would take the goblets down for me and name the patterns over: hobnail, thumbprint and thousand eye, Jacob's Ladder and dark blue Lincoln drape. Her house was full of quiet and beautiful things, family photographs and deep-grained polished oak. I talk about that house so much that one day Bill says, "Let's go there."

He's kidding, I think at first.

"You talk about it all the time," he says.

We are sitting on the deck, sipping Margaritas that Bill made from his own secret recipe. They are syrupy and warm and the sun is hot. The only place we could logically add a deck to our house was on the west side, and, frankly, it didn't do much to disguise the boxiness of the place. It's not much of a deck, either, just unfinished pine cobbled together in an eccentric three-cornered design that Bill dreamed up. We can't use it in the morning because it's shaded by the house and much too cool. By afternoon, the pine is bubbling in the heat, and the deck is like a big, wooden frying pan. But we *do* use it, out of stubbornness.

"It's not that far down to Albion," he says. We live in Des Moines. "I mean, if you're going to talk about it all the time," Bill says, "you might as well go there and get it out of your system."

"It isn't *in* my system," I say. "I'm just talking."

It really is, of course, in my system, as Bill recognizes. He keeps after me until I agree to go. We don't have any kids — no babysitting problems. I keep buying those home pregnancy testing kits with the little paper sticks in them that are supposed to turn blue, but mine never do.

Turn blue. In high school we used to say that all the time. It was sort of an all-purpose curse that was safer to say than real profanity. I ran with a group of girls who were tough and brainy, not the homecoming queens and cheerleaders, and when anyone gave us trouble, we'd say, *Why don't you just turn blue?*

I'm not unhappy. I probably wouldn't be a good mother anyway. It's just that they have so much technology now. *In vitro* stuff and fertility clinics. I go through those home testing kits like M & M's, but nothing happens. Sperm banks. It seems like anything should be possible. I should get pregnant and I should be good at it.

I take a kit with me on the trip down to Albion and use it the second day out, but it doesn't turn blue. Bill always stands outside the bathroom door and sings a medley of songs with blue in the title: "Am I Blue?" "St. Louis Blues," "Black and Blue," "Blue Moon of Kentucky," "Red Roses for a Blue Lady." His repertoire is endless.

I went out with a guy once who called himself the World's First Light Environmentalist. He collected light bulbs and went around the country evaluating the "lightscapes" of big cities and advising the city fathers on what sort of lighting they ought to put in — he got grants for this. He sent me a postcard once that read: *Chicago is orange, about to turn blue.*

He was a cutie, this light bulb guy, but not very bright — no pun intended. I married Bill. He's a high school teacher like me, American lit., but better than I am at it, I think, because he doesn't get so involved. He doesn't expect much of the kids, and they don't disappoint him.

Bill's a lot like my grandfather. He was a lousy farmer, but he knew things. He knew the name of every flower and could imitate the song of every bird. He knew where the deer bedded down at night, and early in the morning, he'd take me there and show me the way the grass was crushed in some secluded thicket. Sometimes the grass was still warm. He could tell you the name of a tree by the sound the wind made blowing through it.

Bill's like that. He knows a lot, has his own private culture, in fact, a selection from the big culture, and Bill is *very* selective. It's mostly old songs, movies and the novels that they're based on, plus Ralph Waldo Emerson, whom he quotes to me in almost every argument. *Being* and *affirmation*, that sort of thing. Bill's a nice guy, kind of old-fashioned, reclusive, the type that has to carry all the grocery sacks and open all the doors. Naturally, he has to do all the driving, too, so I have plenty of time to stare out the window on the way down to Albion.

It's funny, you don't think that land can change. I mean, land is land. It's there, it's permanent. But I don't recognize a thing. It's like a foreign country. I remembered it really hilly, with lots of ground cover and blue pines that smelled a little like gin and made you drunk like gin because, when you were deep inside the forest, the whole earth itself seemed to be breathing. This land is flatter, with almost no pines.

"They probably cut them down," Bill says.

"Why?"

"Timber, kid," he says. "There's no money in trees if you just look at them."

We drive into a swollen town (which I know is Albion only because a sign at the outskirts says so) and drive past a series of vast, sprawling parking lots. A line of fast food restaurants runs along the highway. There's a Firestone Tire Store, a Casey's. We pass a Pamida, a Wal-Mart, a K-Mart, a Sears catalog store holding down a thin line of yogurt shops and poodle grooming parlors called Pineridge Mall. There isn't a pine in sight.

"Keep going," I say.

"What?"

"Let's get out of here."

He swings the car off onto a side street and pulls up next to the curb.

"This isn't what I remember," I say. "This isn't Albion."

"Well, you didn't think it would still be exactly the same?"

Bill is relentlessly rational. A lousy trait sometimes. "No," I say, "no, not the same."

Our car needs a muffler. It's fine if you keep going, but the car fills up with nasty fumes if you stop and let it idle. "Let's just go," I say.

We drive through to the other end of town and out into the country. Set back from the road on an acre of bright green lawn is a pretentious two-story brick house with huge white pillars and one of those little iron footmen with a lantern at the end of the drive.

"There she be, Miss Lady," Bill says. "Belle Reve." An old man is riding up and down the grass on a lawn tractor, leaving neat parallel lines of a lighter green.

The sun is going down. We pass a couple of roadside taverns with red neon signs in the windows and a restaurant called The Happy Chef.

"I'm hungry," Bill says.

"Why would anyone build a house like that?"

For once, he doesn't say anything, and we drive on past similar houses. I project myself inside and inspect their chinzy elegance, the lighted curio cabinets full of figurines and collector plates, the amber swag lamps from Montgomery Ward.

We pull into the parking lot of a motel called The Trail's End. "I'm stopping," Bill says, "before I end up like that guy." He points. A sign over the office shows a droopy Indian outlined in pink neon sitting on a sagging horse. The rooms will have color reproductions of The Lone Wolf and those functional cotton cord bedspreads, not the polyester quilted spreads with mauve iris designs like the Holiday Inn.

We get a room and a meal — a good one — and we stay the night, and when I wake up the next morning, I feel better. We have breakfast, then drive further out of town, trying to find Grandma's old place. It seems to me that there was a lazy S curve and then a road — Turner Road, I think it was called — that snaked away up the hill to the left.

"There was a lake across the road," I say.

"A lake?"

"Well, a pond. And Turner Road, because Gram's mailbox was right at the bottom of the hill where the road intersected with the highway. She used to send me down to get the mail."

We cruise back and forth on a ten-mile stretch of highway, but nothing looks familiar. Then Bill spots a thin veneer of stagnant water on the right.

"That your lake?"

The water is lime-green with algae. A worn tire basks in the sun beside the pond, half-submerged in ooze and looking like an ancient turtle. The sun makes everything glow.

There *is* a road on the left side, Turpin Road, but no hill, no house. "*Turpin* Road," I say.

We get out of the car and wander around for a while, but we can't find even a crumbling foundation.

"You must have remembered it wrong," Bill says. We get back in the car and drive away.

"Turpin Road," I say. "That had to be it."

"Memory's funny," Bill says. "Everything always seems clear. Then you find out you're way off. Nothing's like you remember it."

"That's it," I say. "I know that's the place."

"You never give up, do you?" Bill says.

A billboard begins to swell on my side of the road: *Pioneer Village — 12 miles.* "I remember that," I say. "It's authentic. Everything is pioneer vintage."

"Sure," Bill says.

"Really. We used to go there when I was a kid. It's a real little town. People live there. They live like pioneers."

Another sign pops up: *Pioneer Village, live demonstrations, A Living History of America's Past.*

"I'm not going," Bill says.

◇

But we do go. I insist on it. I want to see if they still make apple dolls and wooden baskets and if Pioneer Village is the way I remember it. We pay five dollars at the gate and drive through. It's almost noon and the sun is merciless on the white gravel of the parking lot.

"I'll give this place one hour," Bill says.

We head down the main street. "I remember this stuff," I say. "I remember the school and the sod house." The general store is now a restaurant with the stale, greasy odor of french fries seeping through the screen door. "Everything looks so much smaller," I say.

Bill is amused. "It's deja vu all over again," he says. "It's the back lot at Monogram Pictures, and — yes! There's Johnny Mack Brown chasing the same heartless villains past the same old tree."

We enter the museum and, trailing along in a line of other tourists, look over the glass cases full of old documents and coins. We look at the dull-colored clothing and blunt boots the pioneers wore, too small for any of us now, and at the random collection of household utensils and tools. It's dusty and hot, and at the first chance we get, Bill and I duck out a side door.

"I'm not much on museums," he says. "I mean, they're like 'so what?' When things were different, things were different."

We wander over to the church and step inside. There are rough, log benches and a simple altar with a pottery chalice that is clearly not meant to be used. The windows are a pale, opaque amber that makes the church seem halfhearted and sad.

"Nothing's like it was," I say. "That museum wouldn't even make a good rummage sale."

Bill says nothing.

"My grandmother had better glass than that. She had a Sandwich Crown paperweight and another one with a poinsettia on a latticinio background that she kept right on her desk. They were rarer than anything in that *museum*."

"So what happened to them?" Bill asks.

"I don't know. She had art glass, too. Lots of it. Signed."

We sit in silence, staring at the discouraging altar.

"Yes, I do too know," I say. "I remember. When Grandfather died, everyone wanted Gram to move to a nursing home, but she wouldn't do it. They kept nagging her, but she wouldn't go."

"She wanted to keep her stuff," Bill says. "Her glass and her piano and stuff."

"I guess so," I say. "Sure. Anyway, when Gram had her stroke and was in the hospital, Aunt Mildred came in with an auctioneer — just to appraise the stuff, you know?"

"Getting ready for the old girl to croak," Bill says. He's met my aunt.

"Right and, anyway, the next time she went back to check on the house, all the good stuff was gone."

"The auctioneer," Bill says.

"Well, we never could prove anything."

◊

By now, it is after three o'clock. The crowd has thinned out, and the sun has darkened to a rich orange shade. We wander into a huge barn. Work lights have been clamped to the rafters. I remember barns as dark and musty, places where I could hide away and dream, but the lights here make this barn as bright as a shopping mall. There are no animals, of course, except one fading fiberglass Hereford, which stares out morosely from the gloom of a stall. Picture displays line the walls, but nobody reads the captions.

A college girl with a deep salon tan is standing beside a big iron kettle and rattling on about how the pioneers made soap.

"I happen to know that the pioneers did not use soap," Bill whispers to me. "This is, in fact, what killed off the buffalo and subdued the red man. The stench that won the West."

The girl finishes and a smiling boy, also tan, comes forward to demonstrate rope-making.

"Thdrese two are made for each other," Bill says. "You are about to witness the historic discovery of soap-on-a-rope."

Having taken a place directly in front of the demonstration, Bill and I have no graceful way to escape. We stand through rope-making, horse shoeing and a detailed history of barbed wire.

The girl comes back, this time making braided rugs. Her voice trills on about the average pioneer woman's typical day. It's an endless recital of drudgery: baking bread, beating rugs, collecting eggs for the egg money, dispensing wisdom and homey folk remedies to her ailing kinfolk, reading the seed catalog by lamplight and darning socks by the dozen. Bill begins to croon "Try a Little Tenderness."

When the girl finishes there is scattered applause. A heavy-set middle-aged woman in running shoes has cornered the boy and girl and is asking detailed questions. Obviously a teacher, she has an enormous functional handbag and a notebook, and she nods her round, gray head vigorously as the kids talk.

"Care to sashay over to the chuck wagon?" Bill asks.

"This is really disappointing," I say.

"If you don't sashay, Ma'am, we could always mosey."

"You have the wrong frame of reference," I say. "This is pioneer. You're doing *Bonanza*."

"I'm doing Monogram Pictures," he says, "where the scenery is forever."

"And nothing's ever for real," I say, "and that's just what you want."

He pretends I'm not being personal. "So, it's tacky," he says, following me out into the sunlight. "Take it for what it is."

"Those kids heard you, you know."

"Naw," he says. "Anyway, they're just actors. It's not like they're really pioneers."

"Well, you're not really Woody Allen either," I say.

He stops walking and looks at me.

"Or whoever you're trying to be. You're not really that funny, you know."

He doesn't say anything. That's always the worst, that's how I know when I've hurt him.

"I'm sorry," I say.

"Okay."

"I really am."

"Don't drag it out," he says. "It's okay."

What he doesn't say — and this is because he's seen a lot of old movies and knows a corny line when he hears one — is: *You used to think I was funny. I used to make you laugh, . . . remember?*

In fact, I do remember and, yes, he did make me laugh and one of the reasons he doesn't anymore is that I know all his lines. What else I know, being an English teacher and therefore skilled in analysis, is that his humor is no longer open and joyous but mechanical and slightly — getting more so every day — defensive. He doesn't want there to be a Pioneer Village and, of course, neither do I — not this way — except that I want there to be something beyond old movies and Emerson's essays and he doesn't. *Life invests itself with inevitable conditions*, he sometimes says to me, quoting Emerson, *which the unwise seek to dodge.*

"Let's go back to the car," I say. "I want to stop at a drug store on the way home."

He puts his hand on my arm. It's very theatrical, almost *Casablanca*. "Do me a favor," he says. "Don't stop at any more drug stores."

I don't understand him at first.

"This is where we are," he says. "And this is all there is."

He lifts his right hand, his index finger pointing toward heaven. " 'Thereby he is driven to entertain himself alone,' " he quotes, " 'and acquire habits of self-help; and thus, like the wounded oyster, he mends his shell with pearl.' "

58

An older couple stops to hear Bill recite, and when he finishes, they smile like proud grandparents. "Emerson," Bill informs them, "*Compensation*."

◊

We compromise between sashay and mosey walking back up Main Street and get an expensive hamburger at the General Store. The sandwich comes in a green plastic basket with a couple of tin ketchup packets tossed on the side and a few greasy french fries. We carry our stuff to a cramped table near the back and sit down to eat.

"You know that song," I say. I'm still thinking of Albion, the way it used to be when I was a kid and my family drove down here every Christmas and the pines were frosted with snow. "About cutting down trees and a tree museum?"

"Joni Mitchell," he says. "Paving paradise." He rips open one of the little packets and thick, blood-colored ketchup seeps out. "But was *this* place ever paradise?" He is teasing. Then he tilts his head and peeks under my bangs to read my eyes. "Maybe it was," he says.

At a table next to us a woman struggles with a two-year-old child over a paper cup full of Pepsi. His face is wet with tears and soda pop, and while I watch, the mother dips a Kleenex in her water glass and wipes him clean with abstract determination.

The sun is butter-colored going down and the road outside the restaurant is veined with the shadows of tree limbs. It's finally cooling off. As the evening comes on, the big horse chestnut trees lose their faded, dusty look and become vivid and dense with color. They seem to swell with life, and the leaves turn a wonderful green.

Cats and Dogs

Sunlight has broken through the kitchen window and rimmed the coffee cups with light. Circles. Utterly simple. Beyond argument. Mike stares at them in quiet fascination. They seem to make such perfect sense. He pictures a tinfoil prophet with blazing eyes, his dusty beard glued on with spirit gum, raising a boney finger to heaven: "I have seen the light on the coffee cups."

A shadow falls over him, and the circles blink out like dead neon. He knows without looking up that she is standing between him and the light, her hands in the pockets of her bathrobe, her eyes probably searching out the pitiful pink bald spot daily widening at the back of his head. This is how the Aztec victims felt when they bent obediently under the stone knife. He imagines his blood spilling happily into a cheap white cup.

"You want some toast or something?" she says. Mike shakes his head. Goodbys are always a drag.

She has a cat that watches them with ghost eyes every night from the top of the bureau. Now it struts on the linoleum, its tail puffed fat, eyeing him in the daylight. Suddenly, it stops. Its eyes go wide. Then Mike hears it, too, the high-pitched whine of a dog, two dogs. A pack of dogs is foraging in the narrow laneway between the apartment buildings. A trash can goes over, and Mike hears the lid cut a hollow spiral, spinning faster and faster with each revolution until at last it wobbles into silence.

"Breakfast," Mike says, meaning the dogs. She — Linda — doesn't pick up on this, doesn't seem to hear him. She scoops up the cat and sits down at the kitchen table across from him. The cat makes a soft, yellow puddle of fur in the folds of the white bathrobe.

"Hello, baby," she says. She cups the cat's face in her hand. "How's the old pussycat?" The cat produces a smile like a looping "w" and flips over.

Mike grabs the newspaper and folds it back noisily to the want ads. He turns the page, making the paper crack. He whistles tunelessly.

She gets up and begins to clear the table. Behind his back, he can hear her rattling the china and punishing the silverware. He hears the pipes shudder and the water rush out like a soft explosion.

"What about a rematch?" he says.

She runs a wet rag in circles over the table, deliberately brushing toast crumbs into his lap.

"I said I was sorry," he says. His voice sounds tinny, pathetic. He stands up and moves toward her. She is washing dishes at the sink. "What about it?" he says. The feeling that he could cry surprises him. He stares at her strong arms and shoulders, shaking the dishes, at the deep hollow between her shoulder blades. "I said I was sorry."

"Stop it," she says quietly. "Just stop."

She turns around to face him with that look she has that has always been able to break him, and whatever it was he was going to say shrivels up and blows away like fine powder. He feels empty and tired and foolish.

"Why do you guys always think everything matters so much?" she says. It seems like a genuine question.

He sinks down on a kitchen chair. The growing bald spot, the monk's mark, seems to rest on his head like a soft, fleshy halo. She runs her hand down the nape of his neck, and he puts his arms around her waist automatically like a child.

"It doesn't always work out," she says. "It's no big deal." She breaks away from him. "Just leave your key on the table, okay?" She walks out of the room.

◊

Half an hour later, he hears the front door slam. He feels her heels striking the concrete as she pounds down the walk, catches the smell of a light perfume trailing behind her. He imagines how her hair swings loose in the sunlight, tossed by the wind.

He wanders into the bedroom and looks around. At night it always seems smaller, warmer. Now the morning sun has sucked the color from the room. Just four white walls are left to hold things together, to keep the double bed from floating away. It's like visiting in an old black and white movie.

She has taken down his poster of the sexy nun, rolled it up and leaned it against his suitcase. The nun is lifting her habit to reveal stiletto pumps and black mesh stockings. Our Lady of Perpetual Desire.

He imagines himself in cool, blue darkness, an old stone church somewhere in Ireland. He imagines rich, green hills in the background. Silent, beautiful nuns scurry over the polished floor. The cross is simple, and the priest looks like Pat O'Brien.

"Father, I . . ."

"Yes?"

"I'm . . ."

"Yes, my son?"

The opium of the people, he thinks. If only it were.

The cat is curled on the bed. A spot of sunlight dots her fur and filters through her delicate pink ears.

"Hello, cat," he says. She blinks up at him.

He sits down on the bed and scratches her head, runs his hand hard down the length of her spine. Her fur is sleek and warm, her body softly yielding. "Good old cat."

She stretches tightly, luxuriating against him; her small, soft paws curl in delight. He strokes her until the friction lifts her fur, then finds the hollow spot between her shoulder blades and digs his nails in hard.

The cat jumps suddenly, spins around and arches on all four feet. Her ears flatten.

Mike laughs and cuffs her ears. "Sorry, kid."

But she spits back. Checking behind her for escape routes, she glares at him.

Mike fakes with his left hand and grabs her from behind, clamping down hard with his right hand at the narrow bridge to her haunches. "I said I was sorry, damn it." The cat whirls and nips him on the thumb, and Mike jerks back.

A pinpoint of blood swells on his hand. A small, red bubble.

Mike swings with all his strength, but the cat is already leaping, mid-air when his fist flashes under her. She bounds off the bed, running, but the toe of his boot catches her square in the guts and sends her sprawling. Mike scrambles after her.

At the closet door, he catches up with her, and she spins around to fight him, but the flat of his hand knocks her sideways and his fingers close around her neck, squeezing hard, lifting her off the floor.

The cat's back legs scrabble against Mike's wrists, and a latticework of dark blood surfaces on his arm, but he holds on. He can feel the delicate bones snap one by one. The energy seeps out of her, and the cat goes limp in his hands, unwinds slowly, sinks like heavy guilt, but he holds on.

◊

Mike grabs a handful of saltines and stuffs them into his jacket pocket on the way out. Linda has left the kitchen spotless, as usual — just their two cups inverted on the drain board, a neatly-folded towel draped over the handle of the oven door.

He walks out the door and down the sidewalk, and he imagines how it will be when she comes home. He sees her kicking her shoes off, opening the mail. She will be wearing the navy blue suit, and she will be tired. When she goes into the bedroom to change, she'll find it, a limp pile of fur like a worn-out muff. He imagines her stooping to look, lifting it up in her arms. He imagines her crying, and he smiles. That's the trouble with pets, he thinks. You just get attached to them and something always happens.

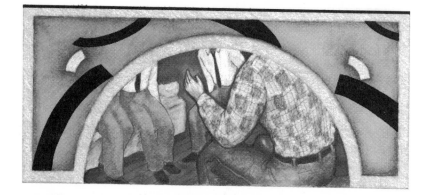

The Bear and The Wedge

Nobody got through four years at Westerlin without acquiring some sort of nickname, except maybe Rhodes, who was too normal to be of very much interest, and me. Most of the names were either assigned by The Bear or fell upon the unlucky recipient because of something someone heard Bear say in conversation. A stubby little red-headed guy named Dave Gassner, for instance, who babbled constantly in a high, childish voice, was renamed Gasser by The Bear; and it was Bear who gave Reynolds the name The Wedge.

"The wedge," Bear said, "is the simplest tool known to man."

The Bear was called The Bear, of course, because of his size and because of his small, close-set flat brown eyes and lethargic movements. He was also called The Bear because he slept through winter term. On the day that the first golden oak leaf brushed his shoulder, Bear took to his rack; and he did not re-emerge — with rare exceptions — until the first high spinning Frisbee sailed past his window in the spring. Tucked in his tossed, narrow bed in Hart House 231, Bear read through the crisp fall, past Christmas and into the new year. He read through the deep, brittle cold of January and the fierce, sudden blizzards of March. Politics, fiction, history, astronomy, philosophy, art.

I was his best friend, his roommate, and together with Gasser and Rhodes, ran the countless errands that knit Bear's life to the everyday activities of the college. I was his exclusive library assistant, for example, spending hours scouring the stacks for the books Bear needed. I typed his papers and delivered them to the offices of his various professors, always with a convincing story about Bear's recurrent illnesses, his complicated class schedule, his dying grandmothers. It was my job, too, to stand outside Sheeler Dining Hall across the quad from our second-story window every evening at four-thirty and flash Bear the news about dinner.

Bear was a fussy eater, and there were few items among the limited round of entres at Sheeler of which he totally approved. He complained not only of the quality, but the quantity of the items offered; and, in fact, the menu didn't vary much. I remember once he tapped my arm during morning chapel — chapel was still mandatory then — and pointed upward at the elaborate design painted on the ceiling. "Written of the cuisine at Sheeler," he murmured. I followed his gaze and found above me an intricate circular emblem intertwined with gothic lettering. "Jesus Christ," it read, "The same yesterday, today and forever."

Bear divided the entres into three categories: brown food, yellow food and red food. Brown food consisted of beef dishes, including his personal favorite, braised sirloin tips. Yellow food was chicken or turkey, egg dishes and macaroni and cheese. These he almost never ate. Red food, at the bottom of the scale, included anything made with tomato sauce, especially the dish Bear had singled out for particular contempt: baked spaghetti. "Spaghetti does not have a crust," Bear said. "It does not cohere."

Since Bear ate only the brown food, it was my job to stand in the melancholy half-light of winter each evening and wait for him to appear at the softly-lit window of our room. If the window was open a crack and the news was good, I'd holler over, "It's brown, Bear," and pretty soon his huge frame would fill the gothic doorway of Hart House. He would amble toward me across the empty white yard, and we would have dinner together, two friends, and talk all night about books and hunting and traveling to Alaska — Bear's dream — and how, even then (it was 1964), you could homestead up north and build your own cabin and stay there all winter and read.

In bitter cold weather, when the window was closed and Bear was too engrossed in his own comfort to open it, I would merely signal: thumbs up, thumbs down. The Bear would take the message and go on reading, and I would have dinner with Reynolds and his crowd and talk about grades and money and other people.

Because brown food was scarce, Bear rarely appeared for

66

dinner. Instead, the small circle of runts and rebels, failed frater-
nity boys and outcasts of all sorts — Gasser foremost among them
— who gravitated toward The Bear for protection made a habit
of stealing food from the dining hall and delivering it to our room
later in the evening. Bear's desk groaned under contraband car-
tons of milk, cookies, baked custards tipped out of their Pyrex
dishes and plopped in a plastic bag, sandwiches, celery sticks, rolls
and ice cream bars that arrived, miraculously, still frozen solid.
When I left Reynolds's table, I'd sometimes grab something too,
an apple, a package of crackers. "For later," I'd say. Like the others,
I did it to gain The Bear's favor, to hear him talk. I lived with him,
of course, but Gasser and Rhodes and the others, they brought
him things in order to be included in his life, allowed to stay in
the warm sheltering clutter of his room, watching his big paws
spinning ideas, feeling safe there. I guess you could say we loved
him.

Like my grandmother played the chord organ, that's how The
Bear used to talk. Bill, I mean. William Joseph Cassidy. His thick
wrists, held chest high, would begin to rotate, and his hands, like
some primitive digging machine, churning out information, would
start to circle, circle. "You know, the whole Jungian thing," he would
say, taking a shortcut, "the whole Marxist bullshit." By depress-
ing one intellectual key, naming one concept, he laid down a full
chord of meaning.

It would have been easy to believe that he was bluffing. That's
what The Wedge thought. He couldn't imagine that a guy on a
football scholarship could have Bear's command of ideas. I don't
think I'm exaggerating when I say that The Bear was brilliant, and
brilliant in a school where high IQs were run of the mill. Com-
petition at Westerlin was savage, and The Wedge was the ace com-
petitor. He was on the offensive all the time, trying to poke holes
in other people's theories, trip them up, or lead them into some
murky mental jungle where they'd be sure to get lost. Bear's push-
button monologues didn't fit into the game, and The Wedge ac-
cused him of hiding out.

I don't think so. I think that The Bear had just acquired so many
facts and theories through his incessant reading that he was, dur-
ing the fall term I'm telling about, in the process of casting off the

details — names, dates, examples — just keeping the main ideas the way a pilot with an overloaded plane might throw out expendible cargo in order to keep flying, the way you lighten your luggage for a long trip. Or, maybe The Bear kept everything. I don't know.

I do know that the talk in our room — Bear's room — on those long winter evenings was something special, and the thing is, was, I knew it then. I knew it. Maybe that's why I never could bring myself to pledge Reynolds's fraternity, although I knew that with my family name, my background, my future, that's where I really belonged. Maybe by sticking by Bear, I was trying to put off becoming the dull corporate businessman I knew I would be one day, taking my pathetic individuality for one last waltz around the floor before the cowardice and conformity that rules our class, Reynolds's and mine, set in for good.

Anyway, because The Bear was a big, slow-moving jock, and because he talked in shorthand, some people thought he was bluffing when he launched into his elaborate explication of *The Wasteland* or rated the merits of Lee vs. Grant. Some even challenged him — The Wedge did more than once — but they never got him, not in conversation. Patiently, in the slow, thick voice The Bear used to talk politics or philosophy, he argued them down, reduced them to children without ever even knowing, I think, that there was an argument in progress. Bear didn't even bother to gloat.

That's the thing that bothered The Wedge the most, I think, how Bear didn't care about winning. The Bear was *pure* somehow. He didn't compete. No good looks, no sports car, no classy blond girlfriend in a navy monogrammed sweater. No ego, no ambition. Just raw, hungry curiosity. The Bear lived naturally, unique in himself, content, tucked inside his own being like a walnut tucked snug in its shell.

To Reynolds, ideas were counters, ways to score, things you knew that other guys didn't know. Winning was everything to The Wedge, and the idea that somebody else could turn his back on victory drove him nuts.

During senior year, The Wedge took The Bear on time after time in class or over the brown dinners or on the rare occasions when he'd stop by our open door just to argue. He challenged Bear subtly, trying to trip him up without seeming to. "So you think Calvin Coolidge was under-rated," he'd say, something like that. "So you feel that the third world can't adapt to a democratic system." The Wedge kept trying for answers, final statements, while The Bear was freewheeling. Eventually, Reynolds's endless arguing got to be a drag. It slowed The Bear down.

"Don't answer him, Bear," Gasser would say. "He's just trying to suck you in."

"Why don't you go read Robert's *Rules of Order*," I said to him once. Reynolds was a debater, a parliamentarian. "Go draw up a charter or draft some guidelines or something."

"I'd expect an adolescent remark like that from one of these other scumbags," he said, his eyes roaming over the guys in our room. "But, you." He shook his head and turned to leave. "If you ever decide to run with your own kind again, Greg," he said to me, "Let me know."

In fact, I was sometimes a little embarrassed to be seen, not so much with Bear, but with Gasser. He was what Reynolds's crowd called a total loser, and I'm ashamed to admit that I tried more than once to persuade Bear to drop him. He wouldn't, of course, and his loyalty to Gasser — he was always getting him out of some sort of jam or other — drew a lot of flak. Who you went around with mattered.

Reynolds's Bear-baiting might have gone on all year if Rhodes hadn't bought the old fifty-one Ford in late October and had it towed to the parking lot in back of Hart House.

"What you going to do with it, Rhodes?" Gasser asked him. "Going to fix it up?"

"Yeah."

"Think you can get it running again? I don't think it'll run. You better get Bear," Gasser said. "I'd get The Bear to help you."

It was natural to think of The Bear. His old man, Bill Cassidy, Senior, ran a service station in Columbus, and Bear could take anything apart and put it together again. He was the only one of us with any practical knowledge, the only working class guy. He didn't go to a regular prep school like Rhodes and Reynolds and the rest. He was older. He didn't even look like the rest of us. When I was a freshman in a navy blue blazer, trying to get my chino pants and my regulation powder blue Oxford cloth shirts not to look so damned new, Bear was still wearing 'fifties Levis with the cuffs rolled up and white dress shirts to class. During four years, his style didn't change. He wore plaid flannel shirts long before — it must have been the ecology movement, Greenpeace, those guys — whatever it was that made them okay to wear. The Bear still wore a Jimmy Dean jacket when the fad had already started to turn toward the sweet, simple-minded portrait of youth in the early Beatles. He wasn't thin and fine-boned like Peter Davis Stoner Reynolds. He wasn't cool.

He *was* an all-state tackle, however, and smart as a whip. He *was* a state resident. There wasn't any reason why he shouldn't go to Westerlin, no reason not to let him in except the obvious, unspoken one: he wasn't one of us.

Anyway, The Bear knew all about cars, so he and Rhodes set up shop in the parking lot. Late at night you'd hear them, the dull, hollow clink of the wrenches and parts crashing, Bear and Rhodes talking low and the high chatter of Gasser overriding it all. When the weather got colder, they kept on working, building a fire in a trash barrel to keep warm. Bear didn't hibernate that fall. The internal combustion engine had a logic that spoke to him. It was history, philosophy, and art.

The work on the Ford drew in guys outside Bear's small circle. They'd stop by before class, after dates to watch The Bear's big hands turning wrenches. Even Old Man McKeever hung around, probably waiting for Bear and Rhodes to knock off for the night so that he could crawl in the Ford and finish a bottle of Beam. McKeever was a sort of custodian, but none of us ever saw him work very much. He was more of a mascot, really, and I think President Miller just kept him on because he was old and worthless and alone in the world; and in Ohio, people take care of old drunks like McKeever.

Working on the Ford, Bear became more visible than he'd ever been before. "Who's the big guy?" people would ask, though Bear was a senior; he'd been around for years. "Who's the guy with the 'fifties haircut?" they'd ask. "Where'd he come from?" Of course, Bear and Rhodes weren't lucky enough to escape the notice of The Wedge either.

"Oh, Mr. Junkman," Reynolds called out in a high, girlish voice the first time he saw the disemboweled Ford spread out on the gravel of the parking lot. "Am I too late for the garbage?"

"You are the garbage," Rhodes said. "Take a hike."

"I didn't know you had your own menial, Rhodes." Reynolds pretended to study the jacked-up car. "What's this pile of shit?"

"For your information, Reynolds," Rhodes said, looking straight up into Reynolds's cold blue eyes. "This just happens to be a classic."

Reynolds kicked the jack lightly.

"Watch it, Wedge," Rhodes shouted. Bear was under the car.

"I don't care what it is, get rid of it," Reynolds said.

"Oh, yeah? Who says?"

"Rhodes, you forget yourself." Reynolds paced slowly around the car. "I'm Class President. The guys elected me to run things." He stopped at the driver's side where Bear's feet stuck out from under the car. "And I say, the President says, move it."

Reynolds walked away.

"That jerk," Rhodes said. "Who does he think he is?"

"He thinks he's the President," Bear said, dragging himself free.

◊

After that, the sides were drawn between the guys who wanted the car moved out of the parking lot — Reynolds's crowd, which was most of the school — and the guys — Rhodes, Bear, Gasser and one or two others — who wanted it left where it was. Every day for a week, Reynolds stopped by before dinner and told Bear and Rhodes to move the car. Usually, Reynolds and Rhodes would argue for a while, and that would be it, although sometimes the arguments got pretty intense. Guys took sides; there was a lot of talk. Finally, one Friday night a note was slipped under our door: *Cassidy, Move the car. Or else.*

"Why's he telling us?" I said. "It isn't our car."

"Maybe we better move it," The Bear said.

◊

"No way. No damned way," Rhodes said when we showed him the note. "He can't do anything."

"Maybe we better move it."

"Bear, no way, man. We got rights."

"You don't know these guys," Bear said. "Guys like Reynolds."

"I know I'm not moving my car."

◊

At dinner on Saturday, The Wedge stopped by our table. "Move the car yet?" he asked.

Rhodes didn't even look up. "No, Wedge, we didn't. Anything else?"

"Okay," he said softly. "Okay, you guys."

◊

About ten o'clock that night, I went down the hall to the john and noticed a funny light coming through the common room window. Bear was asleep back in our room. I went in and pushed a window open and looked down on the parking lot. Lights danced over the chalky gravel. Torches.

I ran back to the room. "Bear," I whispered. "Bear." He didn't move.

I slipped on my robe and went down the back stairs. When I got to the first floor landing, I looked out the fire door and across the parking lot. Reynolds — I recognized him by his height and the stiff way he always carried himself — and some others were standing around the Ford. By now, they had lit a fire in the trash barrel. I saw McKeever, too. Reynolds was reading him out about something. I opened the door a crack to listen.

"I can't do nothing about it, Mr. Reynolds," I heard McKeever say. "It's not my job."

Reynolds said something I couldn't hear, and then McKeever said again, "It's not my job, Mr. Reynolds. You want the Physical Plant Department. They got a wrecker."

Reynolds stared into the fire for a minute. "We don't need a wrecker," I heard him say.

He picked up a stick and prodded the trash barrel, and it went over in slow motion, spilling burning paper and hot coals, and just missing McKeever who jumped back as though he'd been shot. The pool of fire illuminated the milling crowd and the dull metal outline of the Ford.

72

I ran for The Bear and met Gasser on the stairs.

"You better get Bear," he said.

"I'm getting him."

The Bear was awake, standing beside his bed and pulling on a tee shirt. He was wearing the same grease-soaked Levis he wore to work on the Ford and buckskin moccasins with no socks.

"They're messing with the car, Bear." Gasser was hopped up. "You better do something quick."

"Is it Reynolds and them?"

I nodded.

"You better do something, Bear."

"Should I get Rhodes?" I asked.

Bear shook his head. "This isn't about Rhodes," he said. He had a funny look on his face, the same look Gasser had, the same one I probably had too, a look of fear.

"Okay, get him," he said, and I streaked off up to the third floor, taking the stairs two at a time with Gasser right behind me.

"Rhodes, Rhodes." We pounded on the door.

When Rhodes opened the door, his eyes were still heavy with sleep. "What the hell's going on?" he said.

Gasser rushed to the window. "Holy shit."

Down in the parking lot, Reynolds's crowd had teased the little trash fire into a roaring blaze. Flames jumped ten, fifteen feet in the air, and white fragments of burning debris spun against the night. In the wavering light we saw Reynolds's flunkies, like an army of soldier ants, scurrying back and forth to the dorm, carrying waste paper and cardboard boxes, even light furniture — anything that would burn — to feed the fire.

"You better cut that out," Gasser shouted down. Heads turned up to Rhodes's window; then a scattering of rocks struck the stone walls of the building; voices jeered from below.

"I'm warning you guys."

"Shut up, Gasser." We tried to pull him back.

"I'll get The Bear," he shouted. "I'll get The Bear on you guys."

"Whoooaaa." A low, taunting moan floated up to Rhodes's window.

"He's going to get The Bear," someone mocked. "I'm scared shitless." There was laughter.

73

"Hey you," Reynolds shouted up at me. "Tell your roomie to come down here."

"Don't do it," Rhodes whispered.

"Yeah, we want to talk to him," a voice called out of the darkness. "Tell him we got a message for him."

I noticed then that some of the crowd was armed — rocks, sticks, ball bats, things like that. Somebody kicked the jack free and the Ford dropped like a body from a scaffold. The front axle sank six inches deep in the dirt. I stared helplessly at Rhodes.

"Just don't antagonize them," he said. "Keep Gasser quiet."

"Send him down, Greg," I heard Reynolds say then in that sweet, sort of British-sounding voice of his, "Or, I'll send my guys up."

"Jesus, they're coming up." Rhodes looked really sick.

"Come ahead, you sons of bitches," Gasser yelled out the window.

"Gasser, shut up."

"I'm getting The Bear," Gasser said, starting for the door.

"Gasser, no."

"They'll find out they can't fart around with Dave Gassner."

He disappeared out the door, and by the time Rhodes and I came to our senses and followed him into the hall, he was gone.

"I'm going to call security," Rhodes said. "You warn The Bear."

I nodded.

"Don't let Gasser talk him into anything."

"I won't."

"That damned Gasser," he said. "It's about time he learned to fight his own battles."

He ran off down the darkened hallway toward the phone, and I started in the opposite direction toward The Bear's room; but I never got there. Instead, when I got to the stairs, I sat down on the top step and thought about the quick thud the car made when it dropped, like wood striking bone, and I listened to the shower of glass falling as Reynolds's guys systematically bashed the windows out of the Ford. I thought about how naked and white Bear's feet looked stuck in those goofy buckskin moccasins, and I was still sitting there when Rhodes came back.

"Where the hell's Gasser?" he said. "Did you warn The Bear?"

I looked up at him. I still hadn't moved.

"Christ, Greg," he said then — I think he was shouting. "Didn't you warn Bear?"

He shoved past me and took off down the stairs, practically flying, and I followed, trotting behind as Rhodes streaked down the second floor hallway and ducked into Bear's room, shouting, "Don't go out there, Bear."

But when I got to the room, The Bear was gone.

"He couldn't have gone out," Rhodes said. "His jacket's still here."

"But he did go out," Gasser said. He smiled triumphantly. "He's out there right now, kicking shit out of Reynolds. Serves him right, too." He sat down on Bear's bed. "Bear'll show him."

Just then there was a roar, like the sound of a thousand million cannons exploding, and a light like morning. I don't think I even wondered about it. I knew.

Gasser streaked out of the room and down the hallway, careening in at the door of the common room. We heard him at the window. "Holy shit," he cried. "Holy shit, oh my God." We followed him. We looked down.

The Ford was engulfed in flames. Fire licked its belly and played in and out of the windows. It swept across the hood. Fire wrapped the curve of the fenders; it rimmed the dash, illuminating something, a shadow, inside. Then the car blew again, erasing every line in a burst of hot orange, and the crowd dropped back, and I closed my eyes so tight I was shut off from everything except Gasser crying, "Oh, my God, oh, my God," and when I opened my eyes again the fire had settled down to a steady, crackling blaze that sent thick, black smoke curling into the night.

◊

I didn't believe the body they pulled out of the Ford the next morning was The Bear. I still don't believe it. I say the thing — you couldn't call it a man — was way too small to have been The Bear; but Rhodes says the burning shrinks them down.

Reynolds told the police that The Bear got into the car to get something — a wrench I think he said — and it went up when some grease rags underneath it caught fire. He said that there was nothing anyone could have done.

I don't believe it. I don't even believe it was The Bear, but

McKeever — no one ever saw him again after that night — and I bet that's what a lot of the others think, too.

Old Man Cassidy came for the body on Sunday, driving down from Columbus in a dusty, beatup Plymouth almost as old as the Ford. They loaded the body in an ambulance. I don't think the old man even saw it. Then they drove back.

It wasn't The Bear. It was way, way too small to have been The Bear.

No, The Bear is in Alaska, I bet, shacked up with some Eskimo girl, reading all winter like always. That's where he always said he wanted to go. Alaska. Where the winters are ten months long.

The Pink Umbrella

Bob put down his coffee cup and called out loud to no one in particular, "Anybody wants to see fireworks today better get to gettin'."

"I do, I do." Jim stormed down the hallway with his shirt tail flying. "I want to see them."

"Tuck your shirt in then," Bob said. "And comb that hair. You look like the Wild Man of Borneo."

"Borneo, Borneo. Where's Borneo?"

"A long way from here," Bob said.

Bob walked over to the screen door and stared out into the yard, and though his back was turned to her, he could feel his wife, Hannah, watching him. It was a habit she had of watching people, as though she expected something. She had their daughter, Ruthie, drawn in between her knees and was pulling the girl's hair back into two tight braids. Ruthie's hair was honey-colored, just like Hannah's had been.

When he first met her, Hannah had been a waitress — just a waitress, she said, but he knew by the way she said it that she didn't think of herself as a waitress. Her waist was slender then, and she had long, tapered fingernails, painted red. She read movie magazines and could tell you every picture Barbara Stanwyck ever made. He was proud that she was his girl, and he used to take her to the movies every night almost, just to show her off.

"I thought you were going somewhere," Hannah said.

Bob stood in the doorway, and sunlight flowed around him and into the room like water. "That radiator's leakin' again," he said.

Hannah said nothing.

"I thought I had it fixed, and now it's all of a sudden leakin' again. We'll have to take some water."

Hannah jerked her head, motioning back over her shoulder. "Under the sink," she said.

Walking out of the sunlight, Bob felt himself shrinking in Hannah's eyes, melting into the turquoise walls of the kitchen. He crossed the worn linoleum and knelt before the sink, rummaging through the cans and bottles beneath it.

"Okay to use this?" He held up a three-pound coffee can. Hannah nodded.

"I'm gonna crimp it in like this." Bob's bony hands forced a V-shape into the tin. "Make a spout."

He stood before Ruthie and her mother, watching his wife's thick fingers weave the hair, and then he turned silently and walked out.

"It's always something," Hannah said.

◊

In the car Hannah was silent, cold in the hot July. They drove for miles without speaking. Power lines twisted above them as they passed. The tires hummed on the pavement, and there always seemed to be water up ahead. Finally they turned onto a dusty back road. They drove past thick cornfields and frail, lonely farms to a little brick town with a limestone courthouse where a carnival wheeled in the sunlight. A line of hawkers and freak shows and souvenir stands snaked around the square. Pennants flew from the lamp posts, and there was music in the air.

"Here, here. Pull in here," Jim shouted. "Here's a place."

"We ain't stoppin' here," Bob said.

The car rolled past the square and down a side street where every house was white. The lawns were trim, and iris and pale green ferns grew around the foundations. Old ladies watched from behind white lace curtains.

"I don't know why I come back to this place," Hannah said. "I don't know why I let you drag me back here."

"Just don't start nothin'," Bob said.

The car pulled into the city park and the doors flew open. Kids were running, people everywhere, and out of the crowd, a high, thin voice announced, "Look, everybody, look. It's Hannah and Bob."

Over by the shelter house the family was camped like Arabs. The women sat at the weathered picnic tables, talking, while the men sprawled on the lawn, propped up on their elbows, paper cups in their hands, eating deviled eggs and fried chicken from a wicker basket. A dark green watermelon sat in a tin tub of water.

Hannah took Ruthie by the hand and marched forward. "Same old bunch," she muttered. "Damned yahoos."

"Here's old Bob," a woman cried. "Give me a kiss, sugar." The woman grabbed Bob and gave him a peck, missing his thin, tight lips as he darted away. "Old Bob's forgot me," the voice said, pouting. "See how you are?"

"Hello," Bob said.

"You don't remember me, do you?" The woman smiled. "The Redwood Cafe. In Marysville? You used to come in once a week or so," she said.

He drove all night sometimes, shivering in the car because the heater didn't work, fighting to stay awake and get to the next town just in time to call on the feed store owners early, before the farmers began to come in with their orders. He was a sales representative then for a hybrid seed company out of Des Moines. If he got there too late, the merchants were busy and wouldn't talk. If he got there too early, he had to kill time loafing around the square or talking a refill of coffee out of the waitresses at the cafe. He didn't like to waste money on a hotel. He slept in the car or sometimes with one of the waitresses, falling asleep and waking all night long, uneasy in a strange bed. He remembered how dust motes swirled in a shaft of sunlight as a new day came in through the thin chintz curtains of some woman's bedroom. He'd leave before she woke up, before she had a chance to give him that look, leave her asleep in the tossed bed, the sheets twisted like a high meringue, the air stale with sweat and cigarette smoke.

"I'm afraid I don't remember," Bob said.

Suddenly, heads turned. *It's Ed and Thelma.* A thrill like a cool breeze shot through the crowd. A glint of sunlight flared behind the trees, and they heard a low, surly car horn.

"Geez, look at that," a fat boy said, a cousin. "Geez, it's a Golden Hawk."

The car glided majestically onto the grass and came to a slow, ceremonial stop. It was a light bronze color and pinched down low at either end. It gleamed in the sun.

"Geez," the fat boy said.

Uncle Ed emerged from the driver's side and stood in the open car door, lifting his hand in a smooth light curve the way President Eisenhower waved to the crowd from the door of the Columbine, the same way Jimmy Durante lifted his beat-up felt hat to say goodnight to Mrs. Calabash.

"Thelma," a woman shrieked, swaying across the grass with a drink in her hand. "Girl, we thought you never would get here."

The men crowded in on the car. "Beauty, ain't she?" someone said.

"Hell, it's the car of the future."

Ed and Thelma strolled among the family. "How you?" Ed asked. Hannah watched them in silence. "How you, Bob?"

"Ed."

Jim tugged at his father's sleeve. "Daddy, can me and Ruthie go uptown?"

Bob looked at his wife.

"Well, hell, I don't care," she said.

Bob pulled his fist out of his pocket and dropped four silver quarters, one at a time, into Jim's hand. "Now, share this out with your sister," he said.

"I will."

"Even Stephen."

"Yes, sir."

Jim started to run, his ankle-high, black and white Keds rising and falling effortlessly, landing with the steady rhythm of a beating heart, and Ruthie ran after him.

"And don't get into no trouble," Hannah said.

◊

Sunlight filtered through the thick-limbed horse chestnut trees and dappled the broad green lawn with patches of shifting gold. Bob pretended to nap in the shade while Hannah sat sulking with the other women and fanning herself with a newspaper. All of that other, Bob thought, was before Hannah. She made him quit traveling. He took a job in a men's clothing store instead and was home every night.

A young woman sat near him, smiling as though in a dream. She wore avocado green pedal pushers and a sleeveless pink blouse that showed the thin curve of her arms, and she rocked a fussy baby in a canvas stroller. She couldn't have been more than nineteen, Bob thought, about the age that Hannah had been when Jim was born, but not as pretty as she was then, not as feminine. He didn't mind not traveling. A man got a chance at a girl like Hannah maybe once in a lifetime.

A flash of brass caught his eye. The parade was forming behind the band shell. Bob could see the red and gold band uniforms and the flower-decked convertibles where girls sat in frothy white nylon net dresses, pulling on long white gloves. Princesses of the Rotary, the Lions Club, the V.F.W. They wore tiny rhinestone tiaras and lipstick the color of blood and they knew exactly how to lift their arms to the crowd and wave their hands, lady-like, from the wrist. Only sixteen or so, they knew how to smile.

"Pretty," he said. Hannah had sat down beside him.

"I guess," she said.

◊

Ed put one foot on the bumper of the little car and smiled. "Beauty, ain't she?"

Bob nodded.

"The Studebaker, Robert, my boy, is the automobile of the future." Ed took his foot off the bumper, bent over and wiped the chrome clean with the elbow of his shirt.

"That a fact?"

"Hell, yes," Ed said. "Look at that glass. Curved glass, see? Curved all around." He ran his hand over the window to show how the glass curved. "You don't see glass like that in no Chevrolet."

"Guess not," Bob said, glancing away, no longer really talking. Hannah was restless.

"You all ought to get you one," Thelma said. She had come up to stand behind Ed, smiling over his shoulder at Bob and especially at Hannah. "They're awful nice cars."

"I'm getting one when I get big." Jim's voice piped up behind them.

"You are, hey? That's the spirit." Ed dropped his hand and ruffled the boy's hair.

"You'll have to save your pennies then," Thelma said.

"Pennies, hell," Hannah said. She walked away, and Jim followed after her.

"Mama, they got a man up there with two heads, I ain't lyin', and they got this machine with this claw kind of thing and you put a nickel in and this claw thing . . ."

"Where's your sister," Hannah asked.

The boy looked up, empty-eyed. "I almost won a pocket knife," he said, "but I ran out of nickels."

"I asked you, where's your sister." She grabbed the boy's thin shoulders and shook him hard. "I can't trust you for one damn minute," she said.

"She was right behind me," Jim said. "And then when I turned around again, she was gone."

"Well, I hope you're pleased, Mister," Hannah said. "She's probably lost."

"She ain't lost," Bob said.

"The hell she ain't."

◊

Bob ran two blocks north, turned left at the corner of the square, and began to comb the streets, piercing through the loose clusters of people and running his eyes down the line of children waiting at the merry-go-round. He circled the Ferris wheel, knowing she wouldn't be there, couldn't be — she'd be too scared. He peeked behind the barkers' booths, lifting the canvas and leaning over the greasy counters to look underneath. At the Wheel of Fortune, a carnie gave him trouble. "Hey, Buddy," the carnie said, laying a thick, short hand on Bob's white shirt. "You ain't allowed back here."

Bob shoved him back. "Get out of my way," he said. "I'm looking for my girl."

He circled the square quickly, ending up back on the corner where he had started, then began traversing the courthouse lawn, checking each bench and blanket and eyeing the people, some of them rough-looking farm boys, drifters, who lounged on the grass.

A line of women in pale summer dresses stood waiting to use

the facilities in the courthouse basement. Their feet were planted tight together, and their hands were neatly folded and held near their waists. From time to time, a woman would emerge through the dark doorway beneath the hand-lettered *Rest Room* sign, and Bob could catch a glimpse of the cool interior of the courthouse, the concrete floor, the wire waste baskets and the green wooden benches. He could hear patches of conversations, a baby crying, and smell the strong green soap in the glass dispensers. Then the screen door would slam shut again, showing a filmy, half-sheen facade, and the line of ladies would step forward a pace as the woman at the head of the line went in.

Bob scanned the line, but Ruthie was not there.

"Excuse me, M'am." Bob approached an elderly lady in a navy blue dress. "I'm looking for my girl." The woman sighed and stretched her neck, looking away.

"She's eleven," Bob said, stretching his hand out shoulder-high as though that would describe her. "She'll be twelve in October."

The woman turned completely away and the other women, too, and a kind of panic took hold of Bob. If they didn't know where she was, who would know? He ran to the head of the line, jerked the screen door open and stuck his head inside.

Women shrieked, scattered in all directions. He panned the line of stalls where ladies' feet were visible below the closed doors, the row of dirty white sinks. She wasn't there. He didn't know how he knew it. He barely looked, but she wasn't there. And she was not at the rides and not at the concession stands.

He bolted away, past the games of chance and the hot dog stand. Ducking behind a parked truck, he was suddenly on the outside and running down the ragged back edge of the carnival, past plywood facades, gray and spindly, past the portable generators and the huge equipment crates, the beat-up vans the carnies lived in on the road.

A hot, panicky love rose in his heart, and as he ran, he imagined Ruthie in a long line of women. She was wearing a dress that was babyish and way too short for her, and as she advanced in the line, she seemed to grow. Her hair darkened and her face grew pale and sombre. He could sense some evil pulling on his girl, some energy shutting down, doors closing, light cut off. He wanted to

83

call her back, but his voice stuck in his throat, and she was gone before he could make up his mind to run toward her.

He slowed to a trot, then a walk. He was winded and weak and the muscles behind his shinbones ached. He leaned against a telephone pole to catch his breath, and that's when he noticed the lady in gold.

She was sitting in an open car door, listening, while a tall farm boy in a worn plaid shirt talked down at her, telling her something, Bob could see, that the lady already knew. Her costume was gold lamé, long, puffy harem pants and a skimpy bolero jacket in pink and gold that left her midriff bare. Bob could see the fragile ribs beneath the skin and felt as though he could circle her slender waist with his two hands easily. She wore a gold pillbox hat and a sheer pink veil that draped her nose and left her painted eyes wide above it, roving and cautious as a cat's. Her toenails and fingernails were painted pink, and gold bracelets hung from her bare white arms. She was chewing gum.

"Aw, Verline, why won't you?" the boy was saying. "I'd take good care of you, honest."

The lady smiled.

"You said you would," he said. Her eyes snapped up at him in surprise. "You said you would right after the Fourth of July. You said you and me could drive to Wichita."

"Henry, I never said any such thing," the lady said. "I never told you that."

The boy dropped his head and kicked idly at the left front tire of the car. "Aw, Verline."

Glancing over his shoulder, he caught sight of Bob, leaning against the telephone pole, watching, and he shouted, "What you want, old man?"

Bob didn't move.

"Get out of here," the boy said. "This is a private conversation."

Bob looked at the lady in gold and she smiled at him.

"I ain't foolin' with you," the boy said, advancing on Bob. "Just turn yourself around and get out of here."

Bob looked at the lady again, and she smiled again. "Don't do it," he said softly.

She shook her head, still smiling. He smiled back at her and walked away.

◊

The Do-Nut Delite machine was housed in a small, red wagon and was nothing more than a stainless steel wheel rotating over a vat of hot oil. When the wheel reached the lowest point, it blew out a puffy white circle of dough. The dough fell into the golden oil and bobbed on the surface, floating. It drifted down a channel of hot oil and at the end, an automatic spatula scooped the white doughnuts and flipped them over, revealing a golden crust on the bottom side. Further along, another spatula, a larger one, lifted them out of the oil and tossed them lightly into a wire basket. A woman's hand picked them up, one at a time, and twisted them in a pie tin of thin white frosting.

Bob watched the machine, fascinated, until the stare of the lady who ran the stand backed him off, and when he turned away, she was there, Ruthie, almost beside him. She was balanced on the curb, walking the thin ribbon of concrete like an acrobat, teetering, her arms stretched wide. Nearby was a souvenir stand where a rainbow of balloons floated in the hot blue sky and brown plush monkeys dangled from slender sticks. A carnie was stuffing plastic pirate swords and crooked walking canes into a wooden nail keg beside a helium tank. The carnie had an antique, greasy Singer and would stitch the name of a customer on the brim of a white canvas sailor hat for a dollar.

When Ruthie saw him, she dropped her arms, stopped and sat down on the curb. Bob sat down beside her.

"You know, your mother's been worried," he said. "We didn't know where you were."

She looked straight at him. Her eyes were blue like Hannah's, that sharp, pale blue that stared right through him. His daughter was almost twelve, and it surprised him that he'd never really looked at her, never sensed her looking at him.

"You should have stayed with Jim," he said, fumbling. "It ain't a good idea for you to be wandering off by yourself."

"Are you mad?" Her voice surprised him. It was an adult voice, a lot like Hannah's, tired and wary.

"I told you," Bob said. "We were worried." He put a clumsy arm around her shoulder and jerked away, surprised. She had always felt slender before, brittle, like a bird. Now her flesh was soft.

Pink and blue and pale yellow umbrellas rimmed the roof of the souvenir stand. They spun in the breeze and hung upside-down from the flimsy tent posts. Umbrellas were stacked like cord wood on the countertop, furled and secured with a fragile paper band on which red Japanese lettering was splattered like spilled blood.

"How much are them umbrellas?" Bob asked.

"These here?" The carnie pulled one down and twirled it over his shoulder. "These here parasols?"

Bob nodded.

"This ain't no ordinary bumpershoot, cowboy," he said. "This here's a parasol. Direct from Paris, France."

"How much?" Bob said.

"Two, ninety-five," the carnie said. "Genuine silk."

The carnie was short, almost a midget, a toy man with a twisted spine and a mechanical voice. He looked Ruthie over and winked at Bob, and then he lifted one stubby finger to his lips as if to shush them.

He held the yellow parasol high over his head and, swaying it back and forth, he pretended to walk a tight rope, placing one foot slowly in front of the other and teetering, a look of comic terror on his face.

He jumped off the imaginary wire, and tilting the parasol over his shoulder again, he walked with mincing, lady-like steps, peeking at Bob from behind the yellow silk with a wicked smile. He squinted up at the sky and held his hand out, feeling for rain. Then, abruptly, he stopped and snapped the umbrella shut.

"Well?" the carnie said.

"I guess I'll take one," Bob said.

The carnie smiled his crooked smile at Ruth. "Here you go, girlie," he said. "Pink for you. Pink like a rosebud. Ain't that pretty?"

Ruth took the umbrella.

"She's a little rosebud her own self," the carnie said.

Bob fished three crumpled dollar bills from a leather coin purse.

"You gonna have to watch this one," the carnie said. "She's a little rosebud, just about to open."

Bob looked the carnie straight in the eye. "I'm watching her," he said.

◊

"Where you two been?" Hannah wanted to know. "Everyone else is gone."

She looked Bob over carefully, then Ruth. The girl carried the parasol on her shoulder, the way the carnie had done. The silk was a syrupy pink, and the frame was black lacquer. Unfurled, it suggested a big, black spider hidden at the center of a rose.

"Where'd you get that thing?" Hannah asked.

"I bought it for her."

Hannah stared at Bob. "Oh, you did," she said. "And what did it cost you, if I might inquire?" She was swirling a drink in a paper cup. She looked tired.

"Not much."

"How much?" She tossed a strand of loose hair back from her face and looked him straight in the eye. "I want to know how much."

"What difference does it make?" he said. "It's bought now."

"I just want to know," she said. "I'm curious."

Bob looked at the way Hannah's clothes bunched at the hips and the way the flesh of her face had fallen, giving her narrow eyes a sad expression.

"A dollar?" she said. "Two dollars? I just want to know."

He put his face close to hers. "Two, ninety-five," he said. "Two, ninety-five. Two damned dollars and ninety-five God-damned cents." He turned his back and walked away, and she stared at his thin, high shoulders moving into the darkness.

"Well, thanks for telling me," she shouted. "Thanks for letting me know where our money goes to."

The family followed after Bob to the car. "How come I didn't get anything?" Jim said. "I didn't get nothin'."

"Shut up, Jim," Hannah said.

"We didn't even see no fireworks."

They waited at the passenger side while Bob lifted the door lock from the inside. "I hope you're happy," Hannah said to the girl. She held the front seat forward, and Jim and Ruthie crawled in the back of the old Chevy. "I hope you're happy, too," she said to Bob. "Three whole bucks on some chintzy Jap umbrella."

"It's a parasol," the girl said. "It's a parasol, the man said."

"Well, excuse me all to hell." Hannah climbed in the front seat and slammed the door.

Bob started the car and backed it across the parking lot. He switched on the lights.

"Thelma says, 'Oh, Hannah brought her Jello salad again.' Real sweet like," Hannah said. "But, I knew what she meant. She says, 'We brought the ham.' Like nobody knew it. 'Me and the kids get tired of heavy meats, especially in summer,' she says, 'but Ed just has to have it every meal.'"

Hannah pushed her shoulders deep into the seat cushion and lit a cigarette. "'Ed just has to have it every meal,'" she mocked. Bob said nothing. "I'll bet he does," she said.

"I should have told her what me and my kids have every damned night," Hannah said. "We get tired of baloney."

She blew out a thick rush of smoke that rolled against the windshield and bounced back into her lap. "Tube steaks. Know what a tube steak is?" She turned around in her seat to look at her daughter in the back, then faced the road again. "I guess you ought to."

The car wove through the little town and out onto the narrow, dirt road. They followed it for twenty miles or so, then swung onto the main highway, picking up speed. A long, straight road lay ahead of them.

"Daddy?" Jim said. "Do you think a man could really have two heads?"

Bob didn't answer. He wanted to think about the lady in gold, balanced in a hot white spotlight high above a circus crowd, walking carefully on a swaying rope. She wasn't wearing the harem costume now, but a tiny pink satin swimsuit kind of thing, and Bob could look right up her legs to the pink vee that flashed with every step she took. Suddenly, she trembled, lost her footing and started to fall.

"I didn't really see him," Jim said. "I just seen his picture."

Bob said nothing.

"It's sort of a gyp, ain't it?" Jim said. "Just seeing his picture."

The car hummed on. Ruth snuggled down on the worn flannel car seat and stared at the Big Dipper through a side window.

"I should have gone in that tent," Jim said. "I wanted to. I wasn't scared."

"Hush up, Jim."

Hannah twisted around in her seat and swirled a white orlon sweater over her daughter. Ruth was sound asleep.

"I went in the ladies' bathroom today," Bob said. "Uptown." He said it flat, not like a joke.

"What?"

Jim began to snicker.

"I didn't go clear in," Bob said. "I just stuck my head in the door." Hannah stared at him, her head down and tilted toward him, her mouth open a little. One hand held a cigarette halfway to her lips, and she looked like a dime store mannequin. "I don't know why I did it," he said.

"Where at?" she asked him.

"I was looking for Ruthie," he said. "I got confused."

Bob pushed the car up to sixty. "At the courthouse. I didn't go clear in."

Hannah stared at him. He could feel her eyes like a hot beam of light on his cheek, but he didn't turn his head. Finally, she lost interest and looked away. "You're losing it," she said.

The Stone

Winslow inherited the gravestone from his father, Old Jim Moon, who had it carved after one of the several occasions when his drinking brought him near death and inspired in him an elaborate repentance.

Not that he could ever really repent, for there burned inside Jim Moon fierce appetites and a heartbreaking love for the universe that expressed itself in wandering and wild, often self-destructive rages. Liquor triggered Jim Moon's excesses but was not their cause, and, thus, he could never be truly sorry in any acceptable fashion.

Winslow didn't know much more than this, for he knew his father only by reputation. Jim Moon had left Win's mother, then pregnant with their first child, in 1893 to visit the Columbian Exposition. He got to Chicago and just kept going. Two or three weeks later a letter arrived, directing her to name the child she carried Winslow Homer Moon.

The letter said Moon was headed for California and that, when he had made his fortune there, he would send for his wife and son. He never did, however, and the suspicion grew around town that whatever Jim Moon was after had nothing to do with money. Postcards arrived from Utah and Nevada, then Oregon and British Columbia. Jim Moon's wife tacked the postcards on a big wall map she had — she was a third grade teacher — where they seemed like a giant's footsteps tramping the country. They circled around California for awhile, then headed north and crossed back to the coast: Calgary, Winnipeg, Thunder Bay.

Finally, the postcards ceased, and Mrs. Moon and Winslow lived on in town with a kind of invisible mark upon them. They were both pitied and held in awe as creatures whose fate somehow remained suspended. Winslow grew up the way that bread dough swells, out of some ferment inside but without direction. When his mother died in 1913, Winslow was still not "settled."

That the stone was delivered shortly after Jim Moon's death was purely coincidental, but nevertheless it did give Winslow a turn. It came all the way from Winterset, wrapped in canvas, and the stonecutter, who himself drove the wagon, unloaded it with elaborate ceremony.

"I won't accept it," Winslow said.

Winslow did not like what he saw in the stone, and, more to the point, he had no money to pay for it.

"Where I come from," the stonecutter told him, "people shoulder their debts."

Winslow explained that the stone was not his debt, not anything to do with him, but the stonecutter was determined and well-muscled. He showed Winslow the letter Jim Moon had written him, signed in Moon's scrawling hand, and the rough design Moon himself had made for the stone. After some bickering, Winslow agreed to pay the stonecutter — Olsen was his name — a dollar a week until the debt was paid.

◊

"Almost fifty-five dollars," Mrs. Maythorpe whispered. That was a lot of money in 1914. "How will you ever pay for it, Mr. Moon?"

Mrs. Maythorpe owned the boarding house where Winslow Moon had lived ever since he graduated from high school and took the job with Reverend Rayburn as handyman at the Open Bible Church.

"I simply cannot comprehend," Mrs. Maythorpe said over supper, "what in the world your father could have been thinking. A thing like that."

The "thing" was, in fact, a sort of pulpit four feet high, carved in native Iowa granite to resemble a tree stump twined with wistful ivy. Calla lilies grew at the base, and on top — this was the part that made Winslow uneasy — was an open granite book, the Book of Life.

"Wherein," Pastor Rayburn said, passing Mrs. Maythorpe's yard and stopping to comment on the presumptuous gravestone that Winslow had stashed there under the lilac bush, "we may read of our sins and our glory."

Winslow had no sins and precious little glory, unless you counted Caroline, Mrs. Maythorpe's daughter, a girl of modest looks and impeccable common sense, the perfect girl to live a normal life with. Winslow loved her with a desperate hope that far exceeded her merits and would have married her gladly if only he could resolve certain life questions he had and acquire enough money to win over her practical nature.

It was not that she didn't care for him. She did. Win Moon was not the only boy she had ever gone with, but he was cute, she thought, and so serious that he certainly would do something grand with his life once he found himself. They were hampered in their romance by Winslow's poverty and by his legacy, the reputation for lunacy Old Jim Moon had gathered about his family, and now by this unexpected debt beneath which Winslow squirmed like a bug on a pin.

"Pastor can only pay me $6.00 a week," Winslow told Caroline, "And there's my correspondence course and my board." Not being able to afford the seminary in Des Moines, Winslow was taking a correspondence course from the Shipley Institute for Self-Improvement in Chicago.

"Well, Mother says you can't leave that thing in the yard," Caroline said. "People talk so."

"I know."

"Mother says people say . . . Well, you know what they say, and they say that your father . . . Well, Win, he couldn't have loved you very much. Not really."

"I know."

"Or he would have made a home for you, Mother says. That's what people do."

"Caroline, please."

"People don't wander around the world for no good reason and never come home like your father." Caroline was relentlesss on the subject of Jim Moon. "Well, do they?"

◊

In fact, Jim Moon had intended to come home, if he could ever determine where home was. Perhaps he got tired of his own wandering nature and commissioned the stone in the hope that it would one day pin down his ghost for eternity. That was not the way of it, however. Here's what happened.

Jim Moon, visiting New York City, drunk and thrilled by the dark cathedral-like tracings of the Brooklyn Bridge reflected in the shifting currents of the river, stepped off the stern of a Circle Line Ferry tour boat as it passed beneath the bridge. It was a mild day in April with almost no wind, and the tranquility of the scene, bystanders reported, made Moon's action seem understandable. He sank like a stone, almost as if he were diving, and the people who saw him go off the stern reported further that he was quoting poetry — Walt Whitman most likely, although this was not confirmed. Like Ishmael on the mast-head of the *Pequod*, Jim Moon took the water below him for "the visible image of that deep, blue, bottomless soul, pervading mankind and nature." Hovering, as Melville has it, over "Descartian vortices," he jumped.

"He must have been crazy," Caroline said.

"And what does that make me, then?" Winslow said.

"He felt the urge to merge," Pastor Rayburn said, running his fingertip down the blank pages of Jim Moon's granite book as though he were searching for a particularly relevant passage. "And no man dares reproach him." He looked at Winslow.

Winslow did reproach his father, however, egged on by Caroline, and when Moon's identity was at last discovered (through some papers he had entrusted to a girl in a hotel on Forty-Second Street) and he was traced back to his son in Iowa, Winslow refused to claim the body.

"I believe it is in the best interests of all concerned," Winslow had written the authorities, "that my father's remains remain where they are at present interred." He signed the letter "A Dutiful, But Estranged Son, W. H. Moon."

"I think you done just right," Caroline told him. "And as for that old stone, why, we'll just chop it up into gravel."

Destroying the stone, however, proved more difficult than Caroline had imagined. A crowbar, tire iron, and carpenter's hammer all proved ineffectual.

"You need real stonecutter's tools," Winslow said.

She had managed to mar the pages of the book a little and had chipped off the points from the calla lilies, but at the rate she was going, destruction would take her a lifetime.

Winslow sat on the porch steps, watching her work and whittling. "My father only ever sent me one letter," he said. "It said, 'I have named you after a great American painter, and it is my fondest hope that you will live the life of an artist.'"

Caroline stared at him.

"Well, it *is* a work of art," he said, meaning the stone.

"It is a monstrosity," Caroline said, speaking carefully so as to leave no room for misunderstanding, "and the sooner it is rubble, the sooner we can get on with your life." She took a healthy whack at the stone with the crowbar.

◊

Caroline was not able to secure a stonecutter's chisel and hammer. She returned instead with an ice pick, which had minimal effect.

"A sledgehammer," she said. "That's what we need. I think the blacksmith has one."

She stared at Winslow, who, in turn, was staring at the clouds. "Well?" she said.

"What?"

"*Fetch* it," she said. "Honestly, Win."

The sledgehammer did prove effective, but Caroline lacked the strength to lift it more than three or four times, and Winslow refused to participate in the destruction. Consequently, the only damage done was that Caroline bashed two craters in the base of the pulpit and one dead center in the Book of Life.

◊

It was Pastor Rayburn's opinion that Winslow should set up the stone in the churchyard. "You got a pulpit," he told Winslow, "you might as well be a preacher."

Winslow shook his head. "I don't know what I want to be."

"I've seen you," Pastor said.

Winslow blushed. It was true that sometimes, when nobody was looking, Winslow stood behind the pulpit of the Open Bible Church and pretended to preach, silently, to an enraptured congregation. Imagined eloquence rolled out of him, and imagined people stared up from the pews, moved, changed, deeply inspired by Winslow didn't know what.

◊

"Win," Caroline said, "where's Serbia?"

There was a big war coming in Europe, and Caroline talked of very little else. "President Wilson is neutral," she explained, "but people say it's just a matter of time till we'll be in it."

"My late husband fought at San Juan Hill," Mrs. Maythorpe said, seating herself at the head of the breakfast table.

"Mama, he did not," Caroline said. "He was a cook."

"He was a soldier," Mrs. Maythorpe said. "He was right in the thick of it."

"Well, he didn't fight," Caroline said. "Daddy was shot in the head while he was making biscuits," she told Winslow. "Of course, he's still a hero; all soldiers are."

The thought of war made Winslow's stomach flip. "Excuse me," he said and left the table.

◊

Caroline's romance with the war did not distract her from the business of the stone. She continued to work away at it, bashing it, sometimes just in passing, with whatever implement was handy. Every morning she hit it a few licks before starting the day's chores, and she gave it a few more every night right after supper.

"You just refuse to take any responsibility for this thing, don't you?" she would say.

"Maybe we could bury it," Winslow suggested one morning while Caroline was busy abusing the stone.

"Bury it?"

"Maybe we don't have to bust it up. Maybe we could just hide it somewhere, just put it out of sight and not have to think about it anymore."

"Winslow," Caroline said, "we cannot bury a stone four feet long. We'd be digging for days. Besides, it would still be there."

She sat down on the porch step and mopped her brow. "I wish it would sink right down," she said. "I wish it would sink right down to hell." This, of course, was the least of her expectations. "Well, . . ."

"Dynamite," Caroline said, jumping up. "That's what we need. We've been going at this thing all wrong."

"Where would you get dynamite?" Winslow said.

"Oh, I'll get it all right."

Winslow imagined the stone lifting into the air, shattering, and raining down as rubble. "Don't you think that's sort of extreme?" he said.

She looked him straight in the eye. "This thing," she said, "has caused enough confusement."

◊

Winslow Moon was not a well-built man. His arms and legs were scrawny, and he had what the doctor who brought him into the world had called a "hole" in his chest, a deep depression almost the size of a fist beneath his breastbone. Nevertheless, Winslow managed that night to roll the gravestone out of the Maythorpe yard, down the gravel road, and up the little rise past the church. Unlike Sisyphus, he found that, once he got it rolling — he used a two-by-four to nudge it along — the stone tumbled easily, turning and falling in a syncopated rhythm like the beating of a heart.

He rolled it past the graveyard and out into a cornfield where — it was late-July — the stalks of corn concealed it. The field belonged to Eule Seymour, and Winslow reasoned that, by the time Seymour found the stone sometime around harvest in September things might have changed somehow.

◊

"Stolen!" Mrs. Maythorpe yelped. "Win, you should notify the sheriff."

"He don't want it, Mama," Caroline said. She was reading the war news in *The Des Moines Tribune*, her nose close to the page. "Good riddance to bad rubbage."

"I don't guess I'll bother," Winslow said. He was whittling a piece of soft pine into the shape of a calla lily.

96

Caroline stopped reading and pulled her lower lip into a pout to blow her hair away from her eyes. "Well, I don't guess so," she said, exasperated.

◊

Winslow spent considerable time sitting in the bell tower of the Open Bible Church. From there he could see the stone out in Eule Seymour's field. He climbed the tower to think and to pray ferociously for guidance, with his eyes clamped shut and his hands squeezed tightly together. But whenever he got to the part, "forgive us our debts," one eye would invariably pop open, and there was the stone, lying between the furrows, solid as sin with the flat face of the Book of Life open toward him.

◊

"Delmar Avery's going to France," Caroline told Winslow one evening at supper. "He volunteered to fight." She helped herself to more peas. "I do admire a soldier," she said pointedly.

◊

That evening Winslow visited the stone. He set it upright where the moonlight could dapple the pages and leaned against it. Not knowing quite what to say, he said the Lord's Prayer, said it two or three times. He said the Pledge of Allegiance and recited the Gettysburg Address and started in on the Declaration of Independence. He got as far as "life, liberty, and the pursuit of happiness" and stopped. The wind was easing down the corn rows, making a soft whisper in the dark. "Father?" he said.

◊

It became Winslow's habit to visit the stone every evening, arriving just as the moonlight brushed the stone pages and staying well past midnight. He knew now that he would never speak from that pulpit, or any other, but he felt that, if he could just be quiet enough, the stone might somehow begin to speak to him.

One night he had almost begun to hear it when instead he heard a man and a girl's shrill laughter. Trailing the sound through the corn rows, he found Caroline in the arms of Delmar Avery, who

wore a Sam Browne belt, a convenient handle that Winslow used
to wrestle the man to his feet. His strength seemed to come in a
rush, out of the cool night air, filling him up like wine fills up a
bottle, and he felt like he could fling that soldier clear into the next
county if he cared to. Avery had spread his coat beneath them,
but still there was a smudge of mud on Caroline's ruffled skirt and
a guilty look on her face.

"Win, it isn't anything like you think," Caroline said. "Delmar
and me was talking."

Winslow said nothing at first, and the silence stretched out be-
tween them until it was thin and ready to break.

"Well, we ain't engaged," Caroline said. "Not really. And the
rate you're going, we never will get married. And Delmar, here,
he's a volunteer for France."

"'The Moving Finger writes; and, having writ, moves on,'"
Winslow said solemnly. "'Nor all thy piety nor wit shall lure it
back to cancel half a line; nor all thy tears wash out a word of it.'"

Caroline stared.

"Omar Khayyam," Winslow said. He turned his back and walked
away.

"It's a woman's duty," Caroline called after him, "to give a soldier
some comfort."

◊

Winslow was dozing on the sleeping porch when the dynamite
went off. Not really sleeping, he came awake in time to see the
sky light up over Eule Seymour's field. He was too far away to see
the stone heave up and break apart, but he could imagine it rising
over the cornstalks.

He dressed hastily and ran out of the house and toward the road.
From the rise near the church he saw smoke floating across the
road and Caroline and Delmar Avery walking arm in arm and
whispering to each other.

"Evening, Winslow," Caroline said as they strolled past him.
"You're up late."

Delmar giggled. "Thunder probably woke him up."

"Probably," Caroline said.

Winslow raced past them and into the field where only rubble

98

and a muddy crater remained on the site where the preaching stone had been. Chips of granite twinkled in the moonlight, like a map of stars in the mud, and Winslow saw his direction clearly for the first time in his life. Off to the east was the bell tower and Caroline walking away with Avery; north was the road to Des Moines and the seminary. To the south, Winslow saw Eule Seymour, pulling up his suspenders as he ran and swearing loudly to whoever there was to hear him. A lot of corn had been damaged in the blast, and somebody was going to have to pay.

"There is something in art that makes decisions easy," Winslow Homer's father had written him, "directing the mind's eye to the obvious good."

Winslow could not now literally take a page from his father's book, but he was able to salvage one small corner, a pyramid-shaped chip of granite that just fit the palm of his hand. He had it in his pocket later that night when he got a ride to the railroad depot at Creston and caught the midnight train for California.

Beautiful Belle

The two-headed calf was born on my mother's birthday, March 16, in 1939. Mother was thirty-six and I was twelve, and because the incident changed our lives, at least temporarily, I remember it clearly.

I was shaken awake at 3 a.m. and hustled out of bed. "Hurry, Katie," my mother said, "and don't wake the others."

I pulled on dungarees, heavy socks, and the rubber boots I wore to do my chores and followed her out to the barn. It was so cold you could see your breath, and the stars were a brittle, piercing white. I think that even before we reached the stall, I fully expected the unexpected to happen.

The cow was having a hard time, and Mother was talking out loud to herself the way she used to do when she was alone or with me, the only member of the family whom she trusted to overhear her. "Well, Mary Cochran," she might say, dressing herself for mass in a plain, dark dress and pleased, for once in her life, with her appearance, "you're not that bad to look at, after all."

I don't think even Father knew she had this habit. When things went wrong, when corn sold low, when the snow drifted in against the barn doors, sealing off the cows and our one broken-down saddle horse from the feedlot, I would be the only one to hear Mother mutter, "Well, Mary Cochran, you're in a fine mess now."

I sat on Mother's jacket beneath the glare of a single work light, wanting both to watch and not to watch while the cow thrashed and rolled her eyes and Mother, on her knees, kneaded and coaxed and cursed a little, finally *pulling* the calf out of the cow.

It was undersized but well-formed, and if it had not at the last moment made that half-hearted effort to be twins, it might have been a perfect miniature. Mother rocked back on her heels and wiped her forehead, leaving a faint smear of blood. "Well, Mary Cochran," she said. "Will you look at that."

I suppose at first Mother must have thought it would die. She may have even hoped it would, just cease, a mistake, something to be forgotten. So instead of doing what my father would have called "the merciful thing," Mother at first did nothing.

Five minutes passed, then ten, and the calf began to struggle to its feet. "Get the towels," Mother told me, and I ran back up to the house as fast as I could. She had half a dozen old bath towels warming in the oven of the kitchen stove, and when I got back with them tucked under my arm, the calf had its back end standing and was trying to learn to manage its thin front legs.

It kept rising and falling — its own mother would not help it. But when it finally did get its legs underneath it and stood, wet and wobbly, for the first time, it cast its double eyes on Mother with what she, Mother, always called gratitude.

To say that the calf had two heads is stretching it a bit. What it had was two faces, four eyes, two set close together in a worried knot at the center and a third and fourth that seemed to wander, distracted, at the side of either head. There was one broad forehead, caramel brown with two white stars in the middle that reminded Mother, she said, of a double-yolked egg. Lower down the forehead split and became two sensitive noses. A thick pink tongue stuck out of each mouth below.

"Well, life comes on," my mother said. "Whether we like the look of it or not."

Mother draped a warm towel over the calf's heads and shoulders, took another and started to wipe her dry. By this time it was dawn, and Father had come down to the barn to start his chores. He saw the calf, draped in the bathtowel like some coy Spanish girl in a dingy mantilla, but at first he said nothing. He looked instead to Mother, as though she could explain.

"Isn't she beautiful," Mother said. "Beautiful Belle I'll call her."

"I'll get the rifle," Father said.

To a man's way of thinking, it was the obvious thing to do, but Mother wouldn't permit him to kill the calf. She was — and I've thought a lot about exactly what word to use — fascinated. And she was, strangely, proud.

You always feel a bit of pride with every calf, although it's not really any of your doing. But when the birth is difficult, as this one was, and you feel like you're fighting alone in the dark against the mindless waste that is in all death, your loyalty for the calf becomes fierce and stubborn, and sometimes your eyes tear up because of the bravery that is in even the tiniest bit of life. Having fought so hard to bring this calf into the world, Mother could no more have turned her back on it than she could have abandoned me or my younger sister, Olivia, or Glenn, my older brother, or Dillard in his crib.

The cow refused the calf, showing, my father said, more sense than Mother showed. Mother ignored his sarcasm and rigged up a way to feed the calf herself by stretching a piece of innertube over the neck of a Coca-Cola bottle filled with warm milk. She pierced the innertube with a darning needle so that a thin trickle of milk could flow, and the calf got the idea right away. Not sure if feeding one side would automatically feed the other, Mother fed both, and the calf sucked contentedly like any baby, oblivious to her effect on human observers.

My account of what happened next is different from that of my brother, Glenn, who, to this day, recites the story of the two-headed calf with a certain glee. It was the only time in the history of our family, Glenn says, when Mother stood up to Father for any reason. She was ordinarily gentle and obedient, more from a sense of courtesy than out of her nature. She was a wife, hardworking and, when in the company of Father, usually silent. But the calf — this is the way Glenn puts it — just lit a fire under Mother.

Father was not the least bit fascinated. He was not known around Albion as a crackerjack farmer, and the birth of a freak calf was not likely to improve his reputation. We were too poor for the vet bills that Father was convinced would accompany Mother's intention to raise the calf. Nor was he willing, hard up as we were, to feed "that thing," as he called it. He simply could not understand why Mother had kept it alive, and he urged her to let him put a bullet through its skulls.

Mother would not hear of it. The calf was healthy and would

do as well as any other, she said. Furthermore, she was convinced that Belle would bring us good luck. Heaven knows, we could have used some. We could not play God, Mother said, although it seemed clear to her that God was playing with us.

Mother tried to make it seem that raising the calf was simply a practical matter, but of course, there was more to it than that; Belle was my mother's delight. She would sit by the calf's pen early in the morning, before the young children woke — before even Father was up — and late at night, after the dishes were done, and we were at our homework or asleep, and Father was reading the *Albion Herald* or cleaning his rifle or oiling his boots.

What she noticed was Belle-right-side and Belle-left. The calf showed partialities. The right side took the bottle while the left gazed dreamily through the fence, but it was the left side, when Mother spoke, that turned its chocolate eyes to her and seemed to listen.

"We're all a little split up inside," Mother said once, scratching the double star on Belle's forehead. "One side all business, and the other looking away." Although I was sitting there beside her, she wasn't talking particularly to me. Still, I had been privy to Mother's monologues for so long that I understood from that remark both her kind of division and my own. I suppose, like me, she had been a confused and self-conscious girl, wanting to take her place in the world and, at the same time, wanting to take off and run. Even now she sometimes must have caught herself — and Father must have caught her — looking away, although there wasn't much beyond Albion for her to look to.

"It's not looking at anything," Father said. "Probably blind on one side, probably deaf, too."

The calf was not deaf. Mother knew that, but she did not argue.

When the calf was five days old, the pastor came. He wanted to talk with Mother, he said, and he had a thick, worn Bible under his arm, the King James version. The pastor's name was Eli Watts, and he was a big, raw-boned sour bachelor. Watts was Grandma's spiritual advisor, my father's mother; my mother scarcely knew him. He had never been a visitor in our house before; Father would not allow it. Father always said the trouble with Watts was that he never in his life had had a "good time." This, for reasons I could not understand then, always made Mother scowl. Father had ridiculed Eli Watts for years and had refused even to shake his hand, much less attend his sermons. Now suddenly, he had sought the pastor out and was insisting that, in the matter of the calf, Eli Watts knew best.

"I am a Catholic," Mother told Watts, as though that would clarify everything.

Eli Watts did not seem to have heard her. He sat down on the davenport with the Bible on his lap like a box supper. "I'm not saying the good Lord makes mistakes," he said. Watts was a Methodist and not used to irregularities. "But we must think of the poor creature itself. And," he added, "the sensibilities of others."

"If you would care to see Belle," Mother said, half rising from the sewing rocker she sat in, "I'd be happy to show you." The pastor squirmed and declined. "Then, perhaps some gingerbread," my mother said.

Father was not a Catholic — not anything, in fact. He was not a man to take another man's advice, and he had brought the pastor in simply to bolster his own opinion. The two-headed calf was beginning to make him nervous.

Mother, on the other hand, while not without a mind of her own, was usually compliant, so it was not mere stubbornness on her part that made her resist. I think she saw in Belle something familiar, something like herself, but deep below the surface. I saw it, too. She could not have named it, but there was a recognition there, and Mother would not go back on that.

The pastor rose. "Daughter," he said. Mother smiled a little bit at this. "You must let yourself be guided in this matter by your good husband here." He nodded to Father, and Father nodded back, hoping, I think, to indicate to Mother that, between them, he and the pastor had a lock on all wisdom.

"You must think of your children," the pastor said. He took his hat and headed for the door. "If you will not, . . ." His voice trailed off. "Perhaps He will see fit"—Watts tilted his face to heaven — "to remove the mark He has placed upon this family."

It was a good exit line, but not prophetic. A week later the calf was still alive, thriving, in fact, and Mother, who had once hoped that it would die, was now more determined than ever that it should live.

Two weeks before Easter the Catholic church burned down. It was an old church, built mostly of wood, and it went up like a haystack. Mother took this personally, as a sign of the Almighty's disapproval of my father, who would not accept Belle as a miracle. Father, on the other hand, maintained that the fire was, without question, a clear divine message to kill the calf.

"Didn't Dillard come on unexpected," Mother said. "And didn't we think him the oddest-looking baby we'd ever seen, his hair all reddish and sticking up like it does? And Mrs. Melrose in town had a baby with six toes. They didn't kill him."

Father refused to answer her, which was always his way of arguing.

"We don't make the world," Mother said, faltering a little, her logic stretching thin in the void of Father's willful silence. "God makes the world."

Mother borrowed a Brownie Hawkeye and took a snapshot of Belle, initiating her in this way as one of the family, and Father's uneasiness increased. Belle's sweet double face did not charm my father. If anything, it frightened him a little. Father had not been raised on a farm, as Mother had. He came into Mother's land when her father died. He had not seen life close up and sometimes a little skewed, the way farm women see it, and he would not, as Mother would, let nature have its way.

"Volunteer corn shoots up through the beans," my mother muttered. "It spoils the rows. We don't want corn, but the corn doesn't care."

Father Gilley said Palm Sunday mass in an open field just outside of town, and, of course, Mother attended. While she was gone, father put a bullet through Belle's heart, and Eli Watts came by with a man in a pickup truck and took the carcass away.

When Mother got home, the fight began, the first and only one they ever had. It was frightening in its intensity, and it shocked me, what little of it I was able to hear. Emotion was rarely displayed in our family, and this was much stronger than any anger I'd ever seen. Father was furious. I don't remember his words precisely, but he seemed desperate and at the end of his strength, like a man trying to hold the door shut on a strong March wind.

"It's not the calf," Mother kept saying. "It's you, the way you are."

"I am the head of this household," my father said. "And you'd damn well better know it."

"You just can't love anything," Mother said, "that you can't get the mastery over, can you?"

She stormed out of the kitchen, where the fight began, and out to the feedlot. There, seeing the prints of Belle in the mud and the small battered bucket we used to feed the calves, Mother broke down and began to cry.

The next day Mother and I walked over to the neighbor's farm to use their telephone. She called her sister, Peggy, in Des Moines to come and fetch her.

"It would only be for a few weeks," Mother said. "Until I can get my bearings."

I heard Peggy's voice buzzing on the line.

"No, just Dillard and Olivia," Mother said. "Glenn and Kathleen should stay with William." My eyes shot up to hers. "They have two more months of school," she said, telling me as well as Peggy. "And William needs Glenn for chores."

I felt my stomach knot in panic.

"You will?" she said. "When? I'll be ready."

She intended, she told me, to slip away quietly, but that was not the way it happened. Father was coming up from the barn just as Peggy's black Ford coupe turned into our driveway two days later, and Mother was coming out the back door, holding her good yellow hat on against the wind and carrying a brown cardboard suitcase. I was watching from an upstairs window, and for an instant it seemed the three of them formed a long, sharp triangle on the drive. Then Father started to run, and I scrambled down the back stairs. By the time I got out on the porch Father was towering over Mother and shouting something that was lost in the wind and tugging on the flimsy suitcase, which suddenly burst open.

Mother's dark clothing flew up in a whirlwind and scattered over the yard like the miseries from Pandora's box. I sprang through the screen door and ran to help her chase them down, and as the three of us women were gathering clothing and shaking the dust out, Father reached down and picked up a photograph. It was Belle.

Mother turned — this seemed to happen in slow motion — and put her hands out, but Father had already torn the photo in half and in half again, and as we watched he tore the picture a third time and let the pieces trickle from his fingers.

"There will be no more of this," he said quietly and walked into the house.

I chased after the fragments, but I could not find them all. "It doesn't matter," Mother said.

She and Aunt Peggy talked for a while, Mother sitting on the porch steps and Peggy leaning over her, patting her shoulder. Then Peggy got in the car and drove away. I'd never noticed before how lonely the roads are in Iowa, how straight they are, without mercy, without change. Mother and I sat on the porch steps together and watched the black Ford shrink in a shimmer of dust as it traveled straight away from us, never turning. When the car was just a speck on the flat horizon, Mother stood up and went back into the house.

Mother did not know at the time that she was pregnant with her fifth child. When she did know, she seemed to give up her anger, laying it aside like a fancy dress, too young for her now. She told me before she told any of the others, and she used the occasion to tell me, too, about "becoming a woman."

"It's a joy, Kathleen," she said. "You may not believe that at first."

Mother miscarried in her fourth month on a hot Saturday morning. I was wading with a friend down at Win Eddy's farm pond, and when I got home the doctor had come and gone and everything had been — as Father put it — "taken care of."

Father promptly offered to convert to Catholicism, a non sequitur that Mother quietly valued for what it was. She would not accept this "sacrifice," as Father guilelessly called it, knowing that it was insincere and only done to please her, but she did, at Father's urging have young Dillard baptized, the only one of us children to join the church before the age of reason.

Father learned some time later — and this is always the punch line of the story whenever Glenn tells it — that Eli Watts sold the calf to a taxidermist who, in turn, sold it, stuffed, to a museum in South Dakota. Apparently, freaks of nature are valuable to museums, and — this even the mercenary Eli Watts didn't know — more valuable still to carnivals if they can be kept alive and exhibited, as Belle certainly could have been. "Poor Father," Glenn always says. "Mother was right after all."

Glenn believes that the business about the money gave Mother some sort of victory and that, once her anger left her, she was the same as before. Of course, he is wrong. Because he was never privileged to hear Mother's monologues, he doesn't know that after Belle was gone she ceased to talk to herself in the old way, and he has forgotten how for weeks afterward she kept looking down the road toward the point on the horizon where Peggy's car had disappeared in the dust.

Summer passed uneventfully, and fall came. Glenn and I went back to school. Father sold the cow that gave birth to Belle, and Mother began to make plans to raise chickens in the spring. As far as I can recall, we didn't own any more cattle after that.

Thanksgiving was bleak and joyless, and at the end of the meal, Mother announced, to the horror of us children, that she did not intend to celebrate Christmas that year.

"But *you* should celebrate," she told us. "And, of course, there will be mass."

But when Christmas came, she broke her word, drawn — involuntarily, it seemed — into the circle of ritual that the season demanded. She baked the chewy oatmeal cookies that Glenn and Olivia liked and went with us children, Dillard on the sled, to the stand of pines at the end of the south pasture where we always cut our tree. Standing in the fading pewter light of afternoon while Glenn hacked at a scraggly blue spruce, she stared down the road, and the lights from our kitchen, like two pale orange eyes, watched her.

As a peace offering, Father bought Mother a creche, intuiting, almost by accident — for he did not really know her very well — the special joy Mother got from musing upon the nativity of Christ. There was a tiny manger with a crib a little like Dillard's and three wise men who looked nothing like Eli Watts. The plaster Madonna was kneeling, with her arms crossed and her head bowed in submission, and Joseph stood behind her, blocking any chance of her escape. The plaster cows, like ordinary cows, had only one head apiece. They were also kneeling, in so far as cattle can kneel, and it must have been Mother's placing them under the tree that convinced Glenn that things were back to normal.

Someday House

In my memory, it is always summer. I am eight years old, and my brother is twelve, and we live in the house on Delaware Street that my father was constantly remodeling. There the floors were forever bleached with plaster dust, and stray nails and carpet tacks made shoes obligatory in all seasons, all states of dress. My brother and I would go to sleep to the roar of a circular saw and wake to steady hammering, never surprised to find a new half-bath where a closet had been or a door opening suddenly through what had once been a solid wall.

It was my father's dream to live in a perfect house, a house where every closet had a light, where every bathroom tile was stuck down tight, where paint never blistered and linoleum never curled. He wanted every window caulked and every door to shut with a snap, and more than that, he wanted built-in storage space and picture windows and poured concrete patios. He wanted to live in a house that was finished, isolated, self-contained, safe, a place where a man could rest and raise his family; but, of course, he never did. My mother called it the "someday house," our home that was always becoming, never quite was.

My father was a carpet layer by trade, but he started out as a floor sander in the days when houses still had beautiful hardwood floors. Later, when he came home from the war and America was crazy for nylon and plastic and synthetics of all kinds, he learned to set plastic tile and to install the hard, gleaming pink Formica and the bright chrome trim that was everywhere in the 'fifties. He did mostly what he called "commercial work"— restaurants and motels and cheap apartment houses for people who seemed suddenly to be always on the move — and he saved his craftsman-ship for his own home.

In my favorite photograph, my father's hair is still dark. His hands are jammed, self-consciously, in his pockets; an Adams hat tips forward on his head. Staring out from the shadow of his hat brim, his eyes have a half-scared, half-curious look; but there is something about his bearing and about the hat itself that expresses authority.

When my parents went out — just the two of them — my father had a way of setting his pearl gray hat on his head. The New Yorker, I think the model was called, though there was a new Adams hat style every month. He would pull the brim low, slanted over one eye. Then, cupping his hands, he would shape a wedge of hat and air, running his palms forward along the edge of the brim in a twisted salute. The brim would curl perfectly, a part of his pro-file. In the set of my father's hat his whole life seemed balanced, and on the day, years later, when I noticed that he no longer sculpted his hat, that it sat square on his head like a flowerpot on a table, I knew that he was irredeemably old.

In the palmy days, my father owned two cars, an affluence which seemed miraculous to my Hungarian grandmother, my father's mother, who lived with us during the last years of her life. There was the pale blue Plymouth station wagon, rusted out at the wheel wells, with an orange flamingo perched on the hood — my father's work car. And, there was the sea green, impossible three-hole Buick. Riding in the Buick, smelling the clean, plastic efficiency of it, the glue and crisp paint, we were rich and special and isolated from the world of work, as my father intended us to be. They built cars like tanks in those days, and the joy my father took in owning an automobile like the Buick seemed a total justification of what he called "the American way of life."

My father was an independent contractor and did some work for a rich Italian named Cappelli who owned a dozen tumbled-down buildings across the river. The work for Cappelli was most-ly remodeling jobs, chopping up old Victorian homes to make low-rent apartment houses. The buildings were pretty deteriorated; it wasn't always easy to bring them up to code. Cappelli used the cheapest materials and, when he could get away with it, nonunion labor. There was nothing illegal about it, but it wasn't the kind of work my father liked to do.

Cappelli paid his foremen well and in cash, however, and it was nothing for my father to have three or four twenty dollar bills in his pocket, a form of braggadocio that worried my mother sick. She, on the other hand, liked to put every cent in the bank, and in one of the pictures I have of her in my mind, she is washed in the overhead light at the dining room table, a thick green ledger book open before her, a pile of bills on the left hand, a pile of crisp white envelopes on the right.

"Put a stamp on these, Maggie," she'd say, placing a stack of plump, finished envelopes in front of me. I'd lick the stamps and paste them on precisely, impressed with myself for reasons that I did not fully understand. I was part of that elaborate and mysterious ritual which, somehow, kept us safe.

Cappelli loomed large in our imaginations, my brother's and mine, and I think that even my mother was a little afraid of him. Cappelli's black 1954 Cadillac would sometimes cruise to a stop in front of our house around suppertime, and a dark runner would scramble out of the front seat and sprint up the walk with an envelope in his hand: pay for my father.

Cappelli never came in, never got out of the car, in fact. Raymond and I, playing Monopoly on the screened-in front porch, swinging mindlessly to the creaking of the glider, saw his profile, the folds of fat neck flesh beneath the heavy homburg, the glowing tip of a big cigar; but Cappelli was no more to us than a menacing silhouette, a shadow puppet.

"Why doesn't he just mail it to you?" my mother would say. She didn't like the big, black Cadillac idling at the curb. She didn't like opening the screen door to Cappelli's messenger. "It's only an eight-cent stamp," she'd say. "He spends that much on gas."

"It's cash," my father would tell her, sipping a beer before supper. "You don't mail cash."

My father had such energy. It was nothing for him to work eight or ten hours a day, to work Saturdays and Sundays for Cappelli and then to come home at dusk and work another hour or two on his own home. Often, late at night, I would wake and open my bedroom door to see him — sawing, nailing — his shadow fanned up behind him on a sheetrock wall by a harsh work light. My mother would be sitting on a nail keg in the hallway, talking with him, and their voices would float over me as I wandered back into sleep.

My father had a helper named Mickey Tanner who worked with him on the big jobs for Cappelli. Tanner was poor and lived in one of Cappelli's flimsy apartment buildings — he and his wife and daughter — over across the river on Montrose Street. Tanner was a short-coupled Irishman, not very old, not very bright, a lightweight Golden Gloves champion three years running who had taken more than his share of hard punches. His eyes were squinty, and his balance was gone; but he was a good worker. My father trusted him.

Tanner's daughter was what they called a Mongoloid. I didn't know then just what the word meant, except that I'd seen Mongolians in the *National Geographic* — mysterious slant-eyed people wrapped in animal skins — and been impressed by their example with the vast diversity of the world. They lived so strangely and in such a remote place, it seemed impossible that they could share the same planet with me and my ordinary family.

My brother also sometimes helped my father. He was big for his age, and my father let him sweep up on the job and carry material in and out and generally act as a gopher and apprentice. My brother was named after my father — Raymond — an honor which I was convinced he did not fully appreciate or quite deserve. In fact, however, it was the perfect name for him. Raymond and my father looked alike, walked alike and thought alike. They shared, for example, a natural, almost intuitive understanding of baseball and how to play it, and to celebrate the great American game of baseball, my father papered Raymond's room in a wild, gaudy baseball print that ran — bat, ball and glove; bat, ball and glove — up and down the walls endlessly. I pointed out to them that the bats and balls and gloves were all nearly the same size, that the bat could never really move the ball, that the ball could never nestle in the glove; but they didn't seem to think that it was important.

My room, being a girl's room, was papered with flowers: pink roses, full blown, the color of bubble gum. There were endless bouquets of them climbing the walls, each one alike, each caught in a webbing of lace.

Pink didn't suit me. Much to my father's dismay, I clipped pictures of dogs and horses from magazines and tacked them up over my bed, eventually blocking out almost a whole wall of roses. I was not a pink rose girl, not my father's idea of a girl. I was Maggie, a me that I steadfastly refused to let become Margaret.

About my mother in those days I remember strangely little. She was thin and fragile-looking, I remember, and she adored my father; but beyond that, she seems shadowy, a presence more than a personality. Eighteen when my brother, her first child, was born, she must have been about thirty that summer of 1954 when she was pregnant with what she hoped would be a sister for Raymond and me.

The anticipated addition to our family had convinced my father that the simple, two-story white frame house that had served us for almost ten years was now much too small, and he spent hours that summer drawing plans at the kitchen table for a family room. Their bedroom, he told my mother, would become a nursery for Donna, as he had decided to call my sister-to-be; and our living room — too small for a real living room now — would become their bedroom. The new family room — it would be enormous — would be added on to the south side of the house.

The family room became a mental repository for all my father's dreams, a place where he stored not only the architectural treasures he imagined, but his plans for his family. He talked of little else that summer. Of course, it would have a fireplace, he said, and maybe steps leading down from the hallway, creating a sort of split level effect. A picture window — no, bay windows, my father decided — would be set in the east wall to let in the morning light. My mother could have her African violets there. My father said we would play checkers in the family room in the evening and make popcorn in the fireplace. We'd buy a television set, he said.

Some time in July my father brought in a man with a trencher to dig the foundation, and my father and Mickey Tanner cut a dark wound into the flesh of our house, ripping the siding off down to the tar paper in preparation for cutting in the doorway to the new room. Since the roof of the new one-story addition was to echo the pitch of the higher roof on the existing house, they left

113

a tar paper shape like the silhouette of a house, a flat, black outline of a house such as a child might draw.

My mother was against it, or at least, not completely for it. She worried about the expense.

"Ruthie, so help me," my father said. "It's pay as we go." They were talking in the kitchen while my mother peeled potatoes at the sink. My father set his beer down on the countertop and raised his right hand to heaven like a man taking an oath. "No more debt," he told her.

To pay for the family room, my father took on a lot of overtime for Cappelli. We hardly ever saw him, except at 5 o'clock for supper. He'd dash in, wash up a little and change his shirt. He'd bolt his food and then he'd be gone again. On Saturdays and Sundays, he'd be gone before Raymond and I ever got out of bed in the morning, and it would be sundown before he came back.

With my father working night and day, weekends lost their meaning. His Sunday hat went unworn, and my mother stopped cooking her elaborate Sunday meals. Raymond and I hung around the yard, our minds blank and the day looming long and empty; and once my mother, almost out of spite it seemed, packed a defiant picnic lunch and marched us to the park.

"I don't know what you think you're doing," she told my father that night. The picnic had not been a success. "Children need a father, you know."

My father kissed my mother — something we almost never witnessed — and ruffled my hair and played ten minutes of furious, falsely jovial catch with Raymond; but the next weekend he was working again for Cappelli on some low-rent eightplexes across the river.

Sometimes I'd hear them arguing late at night. "Can't you get it through your head," my father would shout at some point, "I'm doing this for you."

On rare occasions, he gave in, turned down the chance for overtime and sat sullen in his big, green chair, drinking Miller High Life out of the bottle and pretending to read the paper. My father was not above raising his voice in order to get his point across, but it was these moments of selfconscious silence I feared more. "Isn't this fun?" he'd say.

Other times he would get the Buick out, and we'd all go for a ride through the steamy August heat. Out in the country the roads were so dusty we had to roll the windows up, and the car would get hot as an oven. "Everyone having fun?" my father would ask.

He didn't mean to be unkind, but something drove him. "Just look at this," he'd say, holding up a chipped coffee cup or a worn bath towel. "See what I mean?"

My mother called worn things "serviceable," but serviceable wasn't good enough for my father. "I've seen it, Ruthie," he'd say. "How they live other places." My father had fought in the Philippines, and what he'd seen there had shaped him, shocked him. He never talked about it. What little Ray and I knew about the war had come to us through our mother.

He was a willful builder, my father, stubbornly hoping that wood and concrete would say what he could not say. When my father's mother died suddenly that summer, he said almost nothing. "We'd been expecting it," he told strangers; but, of course, we hadn't.

I scarcely remember her, Nana, who wore two tightly coiled buns of yellow-gray hair, one over each ear like earmuffs, and spoke with a strong Hungarian rhythm in her voice. I missed her more by the change she made in my father. He had been thoughtful and serious before, a diligent provider. But, he had shown an easy-going humor in the old days, too. He loved jokes, the cornier the better, and he told them with elaborate care, adding gestures and foreign accents if the story required it. After Nana died, he seemed to become harder, less available.

Labor Day came and went almost unnoticed that year. September arrived, and the endless, undifferentiated days of summer became the orderly march of fall and winter, marked by holidays and family occasions: Raymond's birthday, September 25; my parents' anniversary, October 9, when my mother, as round as a melon by then, wore her short, chocolate-colored mouton jacket and my father, wearing his pearl gray hat, escorted her to the Buick for dinner downtown. The room addition was well past the planning stage by then, stalled while my father scraped together the cash for lumber and nails.

Halloween and Thanksgiving came and went, and we were into the swirl of Christmas, shopping and sending cards, wrapping gifts in the traditional red or green tissue my mother favored and hiding them under the bed, behind the furnace in the basement, in the trunk of the car.

My father finished one job for Cappelli and started another. He had long since tacked plastic sheeting over the exposed tar paper; but if bad weather held off, he said, he might still frame in the walls of the family room before the new year. Little Mickey Tanner was still his helper, only now Mickey came to the house every morning and waited, cap in hand, at the kitchen door while my father finished his breakfast. I was never sure why, but my father had stopped driving the Plymouth to the job. Instead, Mickey Tanner drove it, and my father rode on the passenger side. My father had stopped eating his enormous bacon-and-eggs breakfasts, too, and usually just had coffee and, when my mother could bully him into it, toast and juice.

"Mickey, don't you want a cup of coffee?" my mother would ask him.

"Nome," he said. At least, that's what it sounded like he said.

"How's your family, Mickey?"

"Fine."

"How's Peggy?"

Peggy was the Tanner mongoloid. Peggy was the girl my brother imitated, hunching up his shoulders and twisting his face like Red Skelton.

"She's fine," Mickey Tanner said.

Tanner always stared down at the tops of his shoes and turned his cap around and around in his hand. He wore a giant red and black wool plaid coat, frayed at the cuffs. It smelled like coal dust and rotting vegetables. Peggy was not fine.

"Maggie," my mother would coax me, "Say hello to Mr. Tanner."

I always managed to mumble something, imagining Peggy Tanner, her flat, wide-eyed face floating, framed in a window of a decaying Victorian apartment house, a place like the one my father and Mickey Tanner would be working on that morning. Then I would wander down the hallway, littered with sawdust and oddly-shaped trimmings of wood — my father was putting shelving in a closet about that time — enter my own room and shut the door. Enveloped in the heavy femininity of roses, I felt, I suppose, a little superior. I felt, if not accurately defined by my father's house, at least, well-protected. I was in my father's house, safe.

My mother always put up the Christmas tree exactly a week before Christmas, and no matter how much we pleaded with her to buy some new bauble every year, she always used the same old ornaments, the ones her mother had left her, and two or three that she and my father had made for their first Christmas together.

When my parents were first married, it was war time. My father was due to be shipped out any day. There was nothing in the stores, my mother said — she told us this story every Christmas — no colored lights or ornaments, nothing pretty. She and my father did have an old string of Christmas tree lights, but they couldn't find bulbs for it anywhere.

"Necessity is the mother of invention," my mother always said at this point in the story, right before she told how my father found some small, clear glass light bulbs — the kind they use in refrigerators. He secured them in a vise in his workshop and painted them red and pink and coral by hand with my mother's nail polish. "They weren't handsome," she said, "but they were all we had." (In 1954, we still had a few of them; they still worked. My mother used them on our tree every year until they burned out one by one.)

My mother strung popcorn that first Christmas, she said, and cut snowflakes from plain white stationery. It was all they had, until the second year when my father was overseas and my mother's mother, Grandma Vaughn, gave them ornaments of fragile blown glass, several in a heavy maroon color and one with a swirled indentation on each side and one, my favorite, on which three ghostly wise men and an elegant camel journeyed endlessly around the sphere's pale blue equator, following a frosted star to worship a child.

"Be careful with that one, Maggie," my mother would tell me each year. "It was Grandmother Vaughn's favorite."

I had a reverence for that fragile sphere of glass. It seemed sacred. That faded globe, that endless, patient traveling said something to me about myself and my family. It was the roundness — " 'round yon virgin," we sang — and the pale delicacy.

My father did not come home for supper that year on the night my mother planned to put up the tree. He came in late, and I can remember lying in bed, listening to their fighting and staring at the pink rose wallpaper, my eyes weaving in and out of the network of lace.

"Damn it, Ruthie," my father shouted, "I'm doing this for you."

"Oh, no," my mother said. "Oh, no. You're not doing anything for me."

In the morning, my mother gathered me into her grief. She may not have known she did this, but she babied and coddled me outrageously and turned a purely efficient manner on Raymond and my father. She decided that I was ill — the sniffles, she said — and kept me home from school. Then, when my father and Raymond were out of the house, she let the tears slide silently down her face and the two of us sat on the sofa for hours, it seemed, in front of the barren tree, just letting the tears come.

My father came home on time that night, and I could tell that she was glad. When she heard his car in the drive, she ran to the hall mirror. She never wore any makeup around the house, but that night she put on a little lipstick. He seemed glad to see her, too, but he was distant.

"I can't stay," he said.

"Oh, Ray."

"Cappelli wants all the countertops in by Monday so he can get the painters started." He looked away. "Sorry."

"What about the tree?" she said.

"You go ahead." He gave her a weak smile "You and the kids always do most of it anyhow."

I think if my mother had had more drama about her, she might have stopped him from going. If she could have stormed and thrown plates, she at least might have made herself feel better. But she was just not that way. Instead, she sat down at the table and served us our supper, and it was, I remember, the longest and most silent meal we ever ate together.

My father worked late the next night, a Thursday, and then it was Friday, four days from Christmas, and school was out and our tree was still dark and barren.

"All right," I heard my mother say into the telephone when my father called from the job about suppertime. "All right."

We ate without him, and after supper my mother dragged the

Christmas box down from the attic and, silent, began mechanically to hang ornaments on the tree.

"The lights," Raymond said. "The lights go first." He had them strung in a tangle across the living room floor.

"All right," my mother said.

"We'd better test them." Raymond plugged the lights in, and they burst into a fiery nest on the floor. One or two were out.

"Dad always likes the red ones," Raymond said, screwing in new bulbs. He draped the string of lights on the tree and began to arrange them.

"The old World War II bulbs are still burning," he said. "One or two anyway."

"Our first Christmas," Mother said dreamily, "that's all we had, your father and I."

"I'm getting a basketball this year," Raymond said. "Dad said. Regulation. I'm getting a hoop, too. Dad's putting a hoop up on the garage."

My mother and I watched him work, hardly listening.

"You're not getting nothing," he said to me. "You're getting that yucky Christmas candy in your sock, and that's all."

My mother flicked on the radio and fiddled with the dial until choral music, "Silent Night," came in, and then she turned the sound way up.

When "Silent Night" was over, the choir sang "O Holy Night," then "Little Town of Bethlehem," "Away in a Manger," "Joy to the World." My mother sat, watching Raymond struggle with the lights, humming beneath her breath. I had begun to help him.

I suppose at some point she got up from her chair to join us because I remember clearly that she was standing with a silver tinsel rope dripping from her left hand and the pale blue ball with the wise men on it cradled in her right and that she half-turned toward the door when my father came in. I would not have needed to look at him at all to know that something was wrong. I knew from her face and the quick way she turned back to her work and lowered her head.

"Well, well, well," my father said. "Looky here." We didn't know how to speak to him.

"Look here," he said. "Ray? I got something for you."

He was weaving a little, holding a paper sack out at arm's length. "They're new," he said. "They're the latest thing. I got them at the hardware store when I was picking up some screws. They light up."

Inside the bag were three small glass cylinders shaped like candles with red plastic bases and metal screwthreads at the bottom. The cylinders were full of liquid.

"Now, watch," my father said.

He removed one of the old Christmas tree light bulbs and replaced it with one of these "bubble lights," as he called them.

"Watch," he said.

The liquid in the cylinder glowed with light from the base and after about twenty seconds or so, it began to bubble.

"It's the heat from the base," my father said. "It makes the stuff boil or something."

We watched, fascinated, as the bubbles rose in the glass cylinder.

"See? Ruth?"

"They're very nice," my mother said.

"Ah, Ruthie," he said. "You like them. Admit it." He took the pale blue ornament from her hand, grabbed her waist and waltzed her across the hardwood floor. "They bubble, just like you do."

She broke away from him. "I said they were nice."

My father tossed the ornament in the air and caught it behind his back. "Ever see my juggling act?" he said.

He tossed the ornament again, caught it, then balanced it in the crook of his elbow. "Watch this," he said.

"Ray, please." My mother tried to stop him.

"Watch out, Ruth." He was weaving back and forth.

"Don't, Dad," I said.

"A drum roll, please."

The pale blue ball rolled inevitably down my father's forearm, crossed his palm and glided down his ring finger, hung there forever, then fell, and my mother dropped with it, sank to her knees, her arms outstretched like a Madonna, seeking to gather back into unity the fragments as they shattered and skittered across the floor.

"Oops." My father smiled a crooked, wet smile. He fell on one knee and made clumsy scrabbling motions to help her.

"Oh, leave it," she said. "Just leave it."

My father sat down heavily on the floor. "You have to have

something new," he said. He ran his hands through his hair. "Every year. You have to have something to keep you going." His voice was shrill. "No matter what happens," he said, "you have to keep going."

My mother turned her back on him.

My father drew a rumpled sack from inside his coat and held it out to me. "I brought this for you, pumpkin," he said. It was a picture book of horses — Morgans and Arabians and thoroughbreds, all breeds, in fact, with the history of each breed and color photos that showed how they differed.

"When you really love something," he said, "you should learn all you can about it." Then he started to cry.

"Oh, for Pete's sake," my mother said. She circled behind my father, scooped her arms under his and tried to lift him.

"I guess you didn't hear," he said.

"What?"

"I said, you didn't hear." My father had tears running down his face. His hands were limp in his lap.

"Ruthie," he said. "It's burning." He looked up at her, empty-eyed. "It's burning."

◊

The apartment house where Mickey Tanner's family lived caught fire about eight o'clock at night, probably from defective wiring, the newspaper said. Tanner was working with my father six blocks away. They saw the smoke, but by the time they got there, the building was completely engulfed in flames.

"Involved," Mickey Tanner said, telling my mother the story later in the same mechanical if not quite accurate way he had heard it reported on the radio. "The house was involved in flames," he said. "There wasn't nothing I could do."

Tanner's wife and his daughter, Peggy, were dead. Apparently, they had smelled the smoke and tried to escape down a back staircase but had gotten lost in the maze of flimsy partitions and narrow, dead-end hallways in the chopped-up house. Firemen found the bodies heaped together in a corner, the mother's body on top. They surmised that she had tried to shield her child.

◊

After that, my father got old fast. Donna, the dream daughter for whom he had planned so savagely, was born in the new year; but almost as though this, too, were a part of the plan, she died in less than two months. Sudden infant death, they call it, but it didn't seem sudden to us. Donna's death was drawn out in seemingly endless days of indictment, and neither my mother nor my father acted as though they had ever expected her to live.

Ray never got over this. He blamed Dad; and for a long time — most of his life, in fact — kept spinning out explanations of why our father's dream family had failed to thrive. He told story after story about his childhood, or, more precisely, he told the same story, each time with a different slant. He marshalled elaborate political and economic theories according to which Dad was society's victim, then scrapped them for phony psychological analyses or simple, brutal accusations like the one he advanced a few years ago when it was once again Christmas and he was once again blaming Dad for what happened to Donna and Mickey Tanner and everybody.

"If he hadn't always been so damned drunk," he said.

"What?" Ray exaggerated everything.

"He drank, Maggie. Surely that doesn't surprise you."

"You're crazy," I said. I could see my husband, Bill, in the kitchen, pretending to fix drinks, pretending not to hear but with his head cocked at an angle. He didn't want trouble again. It was Christmas.

"He didn't drink," I said.

"That Christmas Eve, just before Donna was born? I suppose he wasn't drinking then," Ray said.

"Oh, sure, he was drunk that night. Why not? After what he'd seen, I mean what happened." The family collapsed of its own weight, that's my theory. Bill says there is no explanation; it just happened.

"He made it happen," Ray said. "He was drunk."

"No."

"Careless anyway. It's the same thing. Those flimsy firetraps Cappelli built. Dad knew."

"He didn't drink," I said. "Maybe a beer or two."

"But I saw him," he said.

122

Bill was standing in the kitchen door with a drink in each hand. "Why do you do this?" he said.

◊

My father died in 1980, suddenly and without any goodbys. He was only sixty-two. Having no one now to worry her, my mother simply retreated into herself and lived on like one of those mysterious air plants that need no water, no sun. My brother had long since gone off to war — except that they didn't call them wars any more, just conflicts — and then to engineering school; and after Dad died the house was sold and sold again, each time to a younger, poorer man, each time to someone who cared a little bit less.

Although he is the namesake, Raymond never made the connection with one place or one human being that would have allowed him to follow in our father's footsteps, marry and start a family of his own. In a backhanded fashion, he is proud of this. When we tell our story — or at least, remember it — he says again and again that he is nothing like his father. I don't contradict him.

He was on the move almost constantly after he graduated. He went to Brazil, all over South America, in fact; he even spent six months in West Africa and, by sheer coincidence, a month in the Philippines near where our father had fought. I have the postcards he sent tacked up on the bulletin board in the kitchen. Ray can design bridges and dams of perfect symmetry, stress balanced and as permanent as steel and concrete get, but he hasn't found that balance in his own life that I used to think I saw in our father — and that perfectly sculpted hat.

I managed it, just barely, though not in the grand style my father dreamed of. Those days are gone forever — that's what Ray says. Bill and I live in a cheap prefab where — by design, perhaps — nothing was made to last. Nothing seems to fit or to have been joined together properly. Doors, for example, hang crooked, swing open by themselves; and when Ray comes for a visit, we sometimes laugh, not very sincerely, about how our father must be spinning in his grave.

Ray always wants to drive down Delaware and see the old house again. I don't mind. The neighborhood has changed a lot since we lived there. Most of the bigger houses have been chopped up into makeshift apartment buildings, and the single-family houses that remain are pretty run down. The evergreen that grew in our yard is gone, and the house itself has been painted a comic yellow. Of course, my father and Mickey Tanner replaced the siding they tore away that summer; but Ray and I still think we see the tar paper silhouette, that childish outline of a house, the ghost of our father's intention, the grand family room addition that never got built in the summer of 1954.

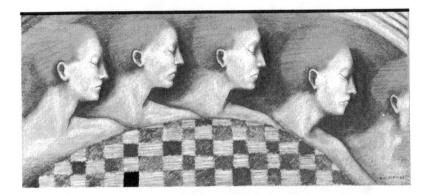

Barbara Croft

is a native Iowan who has worked as an editor, a drama critic, a public relations writer, a journalist, and, with her husband and fellow writer Norman Hane, an out-of-print book dealer. She studied Irish literature at the University of Toronto, where she received her Ph.D. in 1977, and has taught writing at Ryerson Polytechnical Institute in Toronto, at Iowa State University, and at Drake University in Des Moines, Iowa. Her fiction has appeared in *Colorado Quarterly, Poet & Critic,* and *The Kenyon Review,* with nonfiction publications in *Kansas Quarterly, Cimarron Review, Writer's Digest,* and *Georgia Review.* She published a critical book on W. B. Yeats's *A Vision* with Bucknell University Press in 1987 and a textbook on resume writing with Merrill Publishing Company in 1988.

She says: "I'm attracted to writing, I think, because it offers a kind of absolute mental freedom and the opportunity to sort out and to keep what matters. This constant sifting of experience for what is personally and culturally significant is, perhaps, ultimately a moral activity, and, in some sense, all writers are moralists. But, on a more immediate level, writing is an act of affection, and I think few writers write well who do not have a genuine affection for the things about which they write."